The Manager's Guide to Web Application Security:

A Concise Guide to the Weaker Side of the Web

Ron Lepofsky

Apress®

The Manager's Guide to Web Application Security: A Concise Guide to the Weaker Side of the Web

ISBN-13 (pbk): 978-1-4842-0149-7

ISBN-13 (electronic): 978-1-4842-0148-0

Managing Director: Welmoed Spahr
Acquisitions Editor: Robert Hutchinson
Technical Reviewer: Dave Millier
Developmental Editor: Chris Nelson
Editorial Board: Steve Anglin, Mark Beckner, Gary Cornell, Louise Corrigan, James DeWolf,
        Jonathan Gennick, Robert Hutchinson, Michelle Lowman, James Markham,
        Matthew Moodie, Jeff Olson, Jeffrey Pepper, Douglas Pundick, Ben Renow-Clarke,
        Gwenan Spearing, Matt Wade, Steve Weiss
Coordinating Editor: Rita Fernando
Copy Editor: Jana Weinstein
Compositor: SPi Global
Indexer: SPi Global

Distributed to the book trade worldwide by Springer Science+Business Media New York, 233 Spring Street, 6th Floor, New York, NY 10013. Phone 1-800-SPRINGER, fax (201) 348-4505, e-mail orders-ny@springer-sbm.com, or visit www.springeronline.com. Apress Media, LLC is a California LLC and the sole member (owner) is Springer Science + Business Media Finance Inc (SSBM Finance Inc). SSBM Finance Inc is a **Delaware** corporation.

For information on translations, please e-mail rights@apress.com, or visit www.apress.com.

Apress and friends of ED books may be purchased in bulk for academic, corporate, or promotional use. eBook versions and licenses are also available for most titles. For more information, reference our Special Bulk Sales–eBook Licensing web page at www.apress.com/bulk-sales.

Any source code or other supplementary material referenced by the author in this text is available to readers at www.apress.com. For detailed information about how to locate your book's source code, go to www.apress.com/source-code/.

To my wonderful family: Eilene, Steven, Charlotte, and Alice

Contents at a Glance

About the Author xvii

About the Technical Reviewer xix

Acknowledgments xxi

Introduction xxiii

■Chapter 1: Understanding IT Security Risks 1

■Chapter 2: Types of Web Application Security Testing 13

■Chapter 3: Web Application Vulnerabilities and the Damage
They Can Cause 21

■Chapter 4: Web Application Vulnerabilities and
Countermeasures 47

■Chapter 5: How to Build Preventative Countermeasures for
Web Application Vulnerabilities 81

■Chapter 6: How to Manage Security on Applications
Written by Third Parties 95

■Chapter 7: Integrating Compliance with Web Application
Security 99

■Chapter 8: How to Create a Business Case for Web
Application Security 111

■Chapter 9: Parting Thoughts 131

Appendix A: COBIT® 5 for Information Security.......................... 133

Appendix B: Experian EI3PA Security Assessment 147

Appendix C: ISO/IEC 17799:2005 and the
ISO/IEC 27000:2014 Series.. 161

Appendix D: North American Energy Council Security
Standard for Critical Infrastructure Protection (NERC CIP) 165

Appendix E: NIST 800 Guidelines... 177

Appendix F: Payment Card Industry (PCI) Data Security
Standard 179

Appendix G: Sarbanes-Oxley Security Compliance
Requirements 197

Appendix H: Sources of Information... 199

Index.. 201

Contents

About the Author xvii

About the Technical Reviewer xix

Acknowledgments xxi

Introduction xxiii

■Chapter 1: Understanding IT Security Risks................... 1

Web Application Security Terminology 1

Risk Calculation Models 4

DREAD 5

How to Calculate Web Application Security Risk 6

Standard Calculations... 6

A Customized Approach.. 7

Calculating a Security Risk.. 8

Calculating Risk from Multiple Vulnerabilities for Any Asset 9

Calculating the Monetary Value at Risk for Any Asset 9

Sources of Web Application Security Vulnerability Information............ 10

Summary... 11

■Chapter 2: Types of Web Application Security Testing 13

Understanding the Testing Process..................................... 14

Web Application Audits 14

Vulnerability Assessment.. 15

Postremediation Testing 18

Important Report Deliverables for All Testing Reports............................ 18

Summary.. 19

■Chapter 3: Web Application Vulnerabilities and the Damage
They Can Cause 21

Lack of Sufficient Authentication 22

Weak Password Controls..22

Passwords Submitted Without Encryption..23

Username Harvesting 23

Weak Session Management... 23

Weak SSL Ciphers Support..25

Information Submitted Using the GET Method 25

Self-Signed Certificates, Insecure Keys, and Passwords 25

Username Harvesting Applied to Forgotten Password Process..............................26

Autocomplete Enabled on Password Fields...26

Session IDs Nonrandom and Too Short...27

Weak Access Control 27

Frameable Response (Clickjacking)..27

Cached HTTPS Response..28

Sensitive Information Disclosed in HTML Comments...28

HTTP Server Type and Version Number Disclosed...29

Insufficient Session Expiration 29

HTML Does Not Specify Charset...29

Session Fixation 30

Insecure Cookies 30

Weak Input Validation at the Application Level..................................... 32

Lack of Validated Input Allowing Automatic Script Execution.................................32

Unauthorized Access by Parameter Manipulation 33

Buffer Overflows...33

Forms Submitted Using the GET Method..34

Redirects and Forwards to Insecure Sites 34

    Application Susceptible to Brute-Force Attacks 34

    Client-Side Enforcement of Server-Side Security.. 35

Injection Flaws 35

    SQL Injection.. 35

    Blind SQL Injection 36

    Link Injection 36

    HTTP Header Injection Vulnerability... 36

    HTTP Response-Splitting Attack.. 36

Unauthorized View of Data 37

    Web Application Source Code Disclosure 37

    Web Directories Enumerated 38

    Active Directory Object Default Page on Server 38

    Temporary Files Left in the Environment.. 38

    Internal IP Address Revealed by Web Server.. 39

    Server Path Disclosed 39

    Hidden Directory Detected... 39

    Unencrypted VIEWSTATE... 40

    Obsolete Web Server 40

    Query Parameter in SSL Request 40

Error Handling 40

Cross-Site Scripting Attacks... 41

    Reflected Cross-Site Scripting Attack 41

    Stored Cross-Site Scripting Attack 42

    Cross-Site Request Forgery Attack.. 43

Security Misconfigurations and Use of Known
Vulnerable Components 43

Denial-of-Service Attack 44

Related Security Issues 44

    Storage of Data at Rest.. 44

    Storage of Account Lists.. 45

    Password Storage.. 45

    Insufficient Patch Management.. 45

Summary 46

■Chapter 4: Web Application Vulnerabilities and
Countermeasures 47

Lack of Sufficient Authentication 48

    Weak Password Controls.. 49

    Passwords Submitted Without Encryption.................................... 50

    Username Harvesting 50

Weak Session Management... 50

    Weak SSL Ciphers Support.. 51

    Information Submitted Using the GET Method 52

    Self-Signed Certificates, Insecure Keys, and Passwords 52

    Username Harvesting Applied to Forgotten Password Process...... 53

    Autocomplete Enabled on Password Fields.................................. 53

    Session IDs Nonrandom and Too Short.. 53

Weak Access Control... 54

    Frameable Response (Clickjacking).. 55

    Cached HTTP Response.. 55

    Sensitive Information Disclosed in HTML Comments..................... 56

    HTTP Server Type and Version Number Disclosed........................ 56

    Insufficient Session Expiration 57

    HTML Does Not Specify Charset.. 57

    Session Fixation 58

    Insecure Cookies 58

Weak Input Validation at the Application Level...................................... 59

Lack of Validated Input Allowing Automatic Script Execution................................ 59

Unauthorized Access by Parameter Manipulation 60

Buffer Overflows.. 60

Form Submitted Using the GET Method... 61

Redirects and Forwards to Insecure Sites 61

Application Susceptible to Brute-Force Attacks 62

Client-Side Enforcement of Server-Side Security... 62

Injection Flaws 62

SQL Injection.. 63

Blind SQL Injection 64

Link Injection 65

HTTP Header Injection Vulnerability.. 65

HTTP Response-Splitting Attack 66

Unauthorized View of Data 66

Web Application Source Code Disclosed 67

Web Directories Enumerated 68

Active Directory Object Default Page on Server 68

Temporary Files Left in the Environment... 69

Internal IP Address Revealed by Web Server.. 69

Server Path Disclosed 69

Hidden Directory Detected... 70

Unencrypted VIEWSTATE... 70

Obsolete Web Server 70

Query Parameter in SSL Request 71

Error Handling 71

Cross-Site Scripting Attacks...72

    Reflected Cross-Site Scripting Attack 72

    Stored Cross-Site Scripting Attack 73

    Cross-Site Request Forgery Attack...74

Security Misconfigurations and Using Known
Vulnerable Components 75

Denial-of-Service Attack 75

Related Security Issues...76

    Storage of Data at Rest...76

    Storage of Account Lists...77

    Password Storage..78

    Insufficient Patch Management..78

Summary..79

■Chapter 5: How to Build Preventative Countermeasures for Web
Application Vulnerabilities 81

Security-in-Software-Development Life Cycle 82

Framework for Secure Web Application Code 84

Web Application Security Testing 89

    Manual vs. Automated Code Testing..90

    Multilayered Defense..93

Security Technology for Protecting Web Applications and Their
Environments 93

Summary..94

■Chapter 6: How to Manage Security on Applications
Written by Third Parties...95

Transparency of Problem Resolution...95

Liability Insurance as Backup for Transparency of
Problem Resolution 97

Change Management 97

Summary..98

Chapter 7: Integrating Compliance with Web Application Security 99

Regulations, Standards, and Expert Organization Recommendations 99

Government Regulations 100

Industry Standards 100

Recommendations from Expert Organizations 101

Financial Auditors' Favorites 102

Leading Standards and Regulations...................................... 103

COBIT 103

COBIT 5 for IT Security... 104

E13PA and PCI DSS... 104

ISO 27000 105

NIST 105

NERC CIP... 105

Sarbanes-Oxley 106

Integrating Compliance and Security Reporting.................... 106

Summary... 110

Chapter 8: How to Create a Business Case for Web Application Security 111

Assessing the Risk 112

Identifying Risk and Its Business Impact 112

Estimating the Chance of Occurrence of Each Event 113

Qualitative and Quantitative Risk Analysis 113

Calculating Annual Loss Expectancy 114

Calculating the Cost of Prevention and Remediation 115

Calculating the Return on Security Investment...................... 116

Creating the Business Case for Executives 119

Measuring and Cost-Justifying Residual Risk...................................... 122

Calculating Security Status and Residual Risk with a Monthly
Security Health Score 123

How to Cost-Justify and Triage Vulnerabilities for Remediation........................... 124

Noting the Difference Between Remediating and Fixing..................................... 125

Calculating the Cost of Mitigation 126

Measuring the Effectiveness of Mitigation 127

Determining Whether Return on Security Investment Objectives
Are Met... 129

Summary.. 130

Chapter 9: Parting Thoughts.. 131

Appendix A: COBIT® 5 for Information Security............................ 133

F.3 Secure Development.. 134

Description of the Service Capability... 134

Attributes... 134

Goals.. 135

F.4 Security Assessments... 135

Description of the Service Capability... 135

Attributes... 136

Goals.. 137

F.5 Adequately Secured and Configured Systems,
Aligned With Security Requirements and Security Architecture 137

Description of the Service Capability... 137

Attributes... 138

Goals.. 139

F.6 User Access and Access Rights in Line With Business
Requirements 139

Description of the Service Capability... 139

Attributes... 140

Goals.. 142

F.7 Adequate Protection Against Malware, External Attacks and Intrusion Attempts 143

Description of the Service Capability.. 143

Attributes 144

Goals... 145

▓Appendix B: Experian EI3PA Security Assessment 147

▓Appendix C: ISO/IEC 17799:2005 and the ISO/IEC 27000:2014 Series... 161

ISO/IEC 17799:2005... 161

The ISO/IEC 27000:2014 Series.. 162

▓Appendix D: North American Energy Council Security Standard for Critical Infrastructure Protection (NERC CIP) 165

NERC CIP Standards Currently in Force... 166

Future NERC CIP Standards... 166

Future Standard CIP-007-5: Cyber Security — System Security Management 167

Requirement R1:... 167

Requirement R2:... 168

Requirement R3:... 170

Requirement R4:... 171

Requirement R5:... 173

Rationale for R5:.. 175

▓Appendix E: NIST 800 Guidelines.. 177

▓Appendix F: Payment Card Industry (PCI) Data Security Standard.. 179

Maintain a Vulnerability Management Program 179

■Appendix G: Sarbanes-Oxley Security Compliance
Requirements 197

■Appendix H: Sources of Information... 199

Index... 201

About the Author

Ron Lepofsky, B.A. SC. (Mech Eng), CISSP, CISM is the President of ERE Information Security and Compliance Auditors (`www.ere-security.ca`). Ron is an active member in ISACA, ISC2, and several online security communities. Ron has written several published articles relating to a wide variety of security topics and makes home-made dark chocolate treats.

About the Technical Reviewer

Dave Millier is well-known in the Canadian high-tech marketplace, where he's been helping customers with their security and compliance needs for over 20 years. For the past 15 years, Dave has focused on growing one of Canada's most recognized MSSPs, Sentry Metrics, where as the founder he created and brought to market the industry-leading security and risk compliance dashboard, theSentry. Dave is continuing the development of this award-winning platform in his new company, Uzado (www.uzado.com).

Dave has presented at many network and security conferences including Network World, Comdex, InfoSecurity Canada, SC Congress, and SecTor (Security Education Conference Toronto), Canada's preeminent security conference. Dave has written numerous articles for security and networking magazines and is often quoted in the press and news stories. Dave was recognized as one of the top eight security professionals you need to know in the GTA.

Dave is a recognized leader in the field of governance and risk compliance and has helped a number of Canada's leading organizations build their corporate security strategies, align them with regulatory and corporate requirements, and then implement strategies to help them "attain and maintain" their overall compliance.

When Dave's not pursuing his plans for world domination, one client at a time, he's an avid (amateur!) dual sport motorcycle rider and loves to spend his spare time off-road motorcycling.

Acknowledgments

First, I would like to express my appreciation and thanks to all my clients, many of whom I have worked with for years. You have taught me much about understanding your needs and how to satisfy them, all based upon the all-important activity of listening. You have taught me how your management views your responsibilities to secure their network infrastructures and applications and how to best articulate your suggestions in terms of their understanding—return on investment.

I would like to thank Dave Millier, Chuck Ben-Tzur, and Assef Levy, a team of information security experts from whom I have learned a great deal.

I am also grateful to the organizations of ISACA and ISC2 for their informative, practical, and highly useful training and certifications.

I would like to thank Experian, ISACA, ISSA, ISO, NERC, PCI, and SANS for graciously extending to me copyright permissions for their content which I have reproduced in this book.

I am grateful for my years as a student at University of Toronto department of Mechanical Engineering, where I was taught critical thinking and project management skills that well prepared me for my career.

My grateful thanks goes to my editors at Apress Media; Robert Hutchinson, Jonathan Hassell, Rita Fernando, and Chris Nelson, and of course to my senior editor Jeff Olson. Jon, Rita, and Chris transformed an immmature draft into hopefully a clear and useful book. My deep thanks also to the Apress editorial board for having the confidence in me to undertake this project.

Last, but most important, I thank my wife Eilene for her wise counsel and for her uncanny instincts that have directed me well in all things. And a special thank you to her for her generous contribution of time and assistance with this book.

Introduction

Executives and security technologists need a common understanding of web application security risks and how to find and fix them. This book provides common points of understanding to enable both groups to collaborate on building secure web application frameworks.

The book translates with simplicity and brevity the technical world of threats, vulnerabilities, mitigation, prevention, and level of technical risk into language that executives can quickly understand.

Similarly, the book shows executives how to express their need to understand cost, risk and risk reduction, and return on investment in terms security technologists can relate to.

About the Book

Chapter 1 explains how to calculate IT security risk, including descriptions of risk-related terms that are applicable. These terms will then be used elsewhere throughout the book. Chapter 2 identifies and explains the various types of web application security audits. Chapter 3 identifies web application vulnerability classes, specific vulnerabilities, and their risks. Chapter 4 covers the vulnerabilities' remediation.

Chapters 5 and 6 discuss the prevention of web application vulnerabilities, including how to manage security of third-party applications. Chapter 7 shows how to integrate compliance to various standards with security. Chapter 8 brings it all together by explaining how to create a business case to cost justify web application security, and Chapter 9 offers some final thoughts.

Appendices A through H provide more details on compliance standards and sources of expert information.

Companion Files

There are several companion spreadsheets which are used in Chapters 1, 7, and 8. You can download them from the Source Code/Downloads tab on the book's Apress web page (www.apress.com/9781484201497).

These spreadsheets are designed for the reader to readily implement the various strategies proposed in this book.

The first set of spreadsheets is used for various calculations of risk in Chapter 1. Another spreadsheet provides a summary of vulnerability classes, specific vulnerabilities, and their remediation and risks discussed in Chapters 3 and 4. The Summary of Risk and Remediation, with Compliance Standards Added table from Chapter 7 also is included.

Finally, the Chapter 8 spreadsheets are calculators of risk, costs, and returns on investment, which form the business case for cost-justifying web application security. These spreadsheets include a template for creating a weighted score of the health of security for any specific environment.

Contact and More Information

I would be happy to answer any questions or respond to any feedback from readers of this book. Perhaps we can implement these discussions into a second edition! Please feel free to contact me at RonL@ere-security.ca or request further documentation on security subjects related to this book at my web site www.ere-security.ca.

Disclaimer

The advice and information I give in this book are of general applicability and may not be suitable in specific applications. I urge managers always to consult their IT security specialists before implementing any security measures. I cannot accept any legal responsibility for any errors or omissions that may be made or information or advice given.

■ ■ ■

CHAPTER 1

Understanding IT Security Risks

There seems to be a lot of confusion about security terms and concepts. This confusion often leads to poor decisions that waste both valuable time and money. A proactive approach in determining the associated costs of potential losses should a web application breach occur would be the first step in creating countermeasures to reduce the chance of such events ever happening. Without a clear understanding of the proper security requirements and the associated costs, security teams are often misdirected in their persuits. This ends up being counterproductive and often ends in poor decisions or no decisions at all.

For instance, I often hear executives say they want a penetration test, when what they really want is a less expensive and more useful vulnerability assessment. Or management will say it wants a security audit report, but they have no idea of what they will do with it, because they are not familiar with the term *risk analysis* in relation to the security of web applications.

This chapter will remediate the terminology problem.

Web Application Security Terminology

The core message of this book is about helping readers to quickly, clearly eliminate risk in the realm of web application security. Chapters 2 and 3 dive right into identifying the key classes of web application vulnerabilities and the business risks they pose. The terms in Chapters 2 and 3 are those used by security technologists to describe elements of security and how they relate to one another.

Prior to reading these two chapters, it will be helpful to review these elements and their interrelationship with one another. What follows are definitions of the most important terms that will be covered:

- **Risk**: Risk is the possibility of loss as the result of a danger or threat. In this context, we mean the loss of confidentiality, availability, or integrity as the result of an IT security threat. Risks are typically rated as high, medium, and low severity.

- **Relative risk**: In the context of this book, relative risk refers to risk severities in comparison to one another, in a specific environment. For instance, the risk prior to addressing a threat will be higher than after addressing the threat. Risks associated with two separate threats are another more meaningful example. Or the results of one type of threat may pose a greater risk than those of another type of threat. When performing a risk analysis, it is useful to allocate values to risk. A person creating a risk analysis will want to use comparative values for various risks in order to offer clarity to business decision makers. So, for instance, an analyst may assign an 80 percent risk to a high-risk situation, but he may assign a 20 percent risk to a lower-risk situation. These risks are relative with respect to each other rather than being absolute in relationship to the entire Internet world.

- **Temporal risk**: A temporal risk is one that changes over time due to changes in the security environment, and is not necessarily directly related to any change to a particular vulnerability. For instance, if a patch to the affected software that removes vulnerability is made available to Internet users, the risk severity decreases as soon as that patch is successfully implemented. Temporal risk is defined for clarity, but this term will not be used in this book.

- **Threat**: A threat is a danger posed to a web application. There are several sources of threats, such as malware, hackers, cybercriminals, and others with malintent.

- **Vulnerability**: A vulnerability is a weakness that is subject to compromise by a threat. For instance, an unlocked door poses the vulnerability of a thief opening the door, but only if it is unlocked. If the door is locked, there is no vulnerability for the thief, who is a high-risk threat if the door is unlocked but a very-low-risk threat if the door is, in fact, locked.

- **Breach**: A security breach is a threat that takes active advantage of a weakness or vulnerability and may compromise the application. In the example just given, a thief actively opening the unlocked door is an act of compromise. A breach is more associated with vulnerabilities.

- **Compromise**: A compromise is a synonym for a breach except the term is more associated with risk. I use *breach* and *compromise* interchangeably.

- **Mitigation**: A mitigation is a repair or a protection made as a defense against a threat. A mitigation either repairs vulnerability or reduces its seriousness in order to make the vulnerability less susceptible to compromise by a threat. Risk is reduced by mitigation.

  As a physical analogy for a logical security problem, we can use the example of an unlocked door to a building. A mitigation for the unlocked door may have three components:

  - Locking the door immediately

  - Making a policy that everyone who opens the door must subsequently leave it locked

  - Making a policy that once per day a designated person checks that the door is locked, always at different times

- **Countermeasure**: A countermeasure is often used instead of a mitigation when the vulnerability simply cannot be removed and a work-around is required. An example is where there are known code vulnerabilities within a web application but the code cannot be modified for valid business reasons. A countermeasure to these vulnerabilities could be a web application firewall.

  However, a countermeasure can also refer to a safeguard that addresses a threat and mitigates risk. A countermeasure is usually associated with a threat and a mitigation is usually associated with a risk. I use the terms *countermeasure* and *mitigation* interchangeably because, in practice, they are functionally equivalent.

- **Residual risk**: Residual risk is the risk that still remains after mitigation. This may sound unclear at first, as one assumes mitigation reduces risk to zero. However, in a situation with high risk vulnerability, there may be reasons why the risk can only be reduced but not completely eliminated. In the analogy of the unlocked door, for example, if the locked door policy is laxly followed and the designated lock checker misses an unlocked door, residual risk arises. In addition, residual risk can reoccur, particularly in a dynamic environment where changes subsequent to mitigation virtually undo the mitigation or create new vulnerabilities.

Risk Calculation Models

There are many models for calculating risk in the area of IT security. What follows is a selection of the better-known risk-analysis methodologies or tools:

- **CRAMM:** An acronym standing for the "CTCA risk analysis and management method," it refers to a process of analysis that combines assets, threats, and vulnerabilities to evaluate risk and come up with a list of countermeasures.

- **DREAD:** "Damage, reproducibility, exploitability, affected users, discoverability" is a Microsoft model focused on vulnerabilities and their outcomes. DREAD comes with a scoring plan that makes creating a quantitative DREAD score straightforward and less qualitative.

- **STRIDE:** "Spoofing identity, tampering with data, repudiation, information disclosure, denial of service, and elevation of privilege" is a model focused on types of threats.

■ **Note**   DREAD and STRIDE are measurement systems that are sometimes used in conjunction with each other.

- **FRAP:** The "facilitated risk analysis process" is a type of qualitative risk analysis focused on organizing teams from business units in order to address security.

- **OCTAVE Allegro:** Developed by CERT, "operationally critical threat, asset and vulnerability evaluation" is a suite of tools, techniques, and methods for risk-based information security strategic assessment and planning. There are two versions of OCTAVE: full OCTAVE for large organizations and OCTAVE-S for small organizations.

- **Spanning Tree Analysis:** This is a technique for creating a "tree" of all possible threats to a system.

There are other risk assessment models, and the reader can pick and choose which components make most sense from each of them. I have chosen to focus on DREAD as an example to drill down on simply because I use this model, as well as STRIDE, in all of my audit reports.

DREAD

The DREAD model is a widely used methodology for calculating the degree of risk presented by a threat. It involves attaching a numeric score to five risk variables and then calculating another score for a particular threat. Information about DREAD is available on the Open Web Application Security Project (OWASP) web page (www.owasp.org).

The five variables for calculating risk in the DREAD model are:

- **Damage potential**: Assesses how much damage an exploited vulnerability could cause. The more damage, the higher the risk.

- **Reproducibility**: Determines the degree of difficulty of reproducing or making an exploit happen. The easier the reproduction, the higher the risk.

- **Exploitability**: Evaluates the degree of expertise, time, and tools needed to execute the exploit. The easier the process, the higher the risk.

- **Affected users**: Calculates the number and importance of users that could be affected. The larger the number and the higher the importance, the higher the risk.

- **Discoverability**: Assesses the ease of identifying the threat, which might range from one that is obvious and is shown in a web browser address bar to one that is not documented and is very difficult to detect. The more difficult to detect, the higher the risk.

You then assign one of the following values to each of the five variables to get a clear indication of the security posture:

0 = Nothing

5 = Medium risk description

10 = High risk description

An example is a cross-site scripting vulnerability, whose DREAD score may be:

Damage potential: 10

Reproducibility: 5

Exploitability: 10

Affected users: 10

Discoverability: 5

Total score: 40

In this case, the reader can infer from the high total score that the vulnerability has great large damage potential to a great number of users and should be mitigated immediately.

How to Calculate Web Application Security Risk

Not to put too fine a point on this, but it is useful to understand how security experts calculate security risk. An agreed-to understanding of the definition of risk among executives and their security teams is a key element for more clear, concise communication. This will be useful in Chapter 2, which associates classes of vulnerabilities with risk; in Chapter 4, which explains how to remediate vulnerabilities; and in Chapter 8, which explains the structure of a business case for justifying web application security. In Chapter 8, actual values of risk are used.

Since executive management teams prefer to think of IT security in terms of risk, currency, and return on investment, it is useful for them to instruct IT security technology experts to translate technical security into language that they can understand. Chapter 8 explains how to do this in detail.

Standard Calculations

I will first look at the standard risk calculation method and then show a customized version. Next, I will use the customized version to show examples of three types of risk calculation:

- Calculating any security risk

- Applying that calculation to multiple risks threatening a single asset

- Calculating the monetary value at risk for an asset

In most real-life business environments, calculations of risk are based upon estimated values pertaining to the technology side of risk, generating estimated values for risk and the cost of risk. Industry experts such as ISC(2) (International Information Systems Security Certification Consortium) and ISACA (formerly Information Systems Audit and Control Association, but now known just by the ISACA acronym) publish equations for calculating risk using the following variables:

- The monetary value of loss associated with the compromise of any specific asset

- The probability that a specific type of security breach/event will occur for a specific asset

- The estimated number of times per year a specific breach/event will occur. This type of statistic may be available from publishers of information on risk. However, it is not easy to gather statistics about security events, as many organizations are reticent to divulge data about their security events.

Annual loss expectancy is calculated by multiplying

the expected loss in $ × the probability of a specific breach × the estimated number of occurrences per year.

A Customized Approach

I have created a slightly different version of the risk calculation, which attempts to estimate the risk of an event by articulating the variables that security technologists live with on a daily basis:

- Any key asset and the estimated monetary loss expected to result from a breach

- The existence of a threat to that asset

- Any security vulnerabilities associated with that asset

- Any mitigation/prevention steps currently being deployed

I believe that a meaningful way of calculating risk is to attach estimated values to each of these variables, with an explanation to management of how the estimates were derived. The values can be expressed in the following ways:

- *As a dollar value for the loss of any key asset.* This is the dollar value at risk if the asset were to be compromised. It could be the cost of production downtime, legal costs, or other costs associated with a loss. This is discussed in more detail in Chapter 8, which identifies how to create business cases involving return on investment. Management is the best source for providing the monetary value of each key asset and the expected monetary loss associated with any key asset.

- *As a percentage value indicating the possibility that a threat exists.* The existence of a threat could be 100% if there is a known threat. However, in some cases the value could be less than 100%, such as if the existence of a threat is predicted but not confirmed.

- *As a percentage value that a vulnerability to the known threat exists.* If there is no vulnerability susceptible to a threat, the vulnerability value is 0%. If a vulnerability is highly susceptible to a threat, the value is 100%. If there is a vulnerability that is difficult to compromise by the threat, the vulnerability is assigned some other percentage.

The confidence level in any mitigation/preventative step is expressed as a percentage value. The value may vary widely depending upon in-house experience, shared experiences among the professional-security world, in-house testing, and security-audit testing by impartial third parties.

Calculating a Security Risk

The steps for calculating a security risk are:

1. *Identify each asset in scope.* Use the following process for each asset.

2. *Identify the existence of a threat to an asset.* If a threat exists, then the percentage value of the threat is, of course, 100%.

3. *Identify any security vulnerabilities associated with an asset.* The percentage represents the degree of risk posed by a vulnerability. For instance, a medium-to-high risk may be 80%, while a very low risk may be 10%.

4. *Identify mitigation steps and what percentage of risk remains after they are taken.* If the mitigation reduces risk completely, then the risk is 0%.

The idea here is that when risk is multiplied by the currency value of an asset, the value at risk will be zero value for a zero risk factor and at the other extreme will be simply the currency value of an asset.

The following equation is an example calculation of security risk. Estimated values for each factor are then given.

$$\% \text{ risk} = \text{existence of a threat to that asset}$$
$$\times \text{ any security vulnerabilities associated with that asset}$$
$$\times \text{ any mitigation/prevention steps deployed}$$

Factors for calculating risk	% values assigned by the security technology team
Existence of a threat to the asset	100%
Risk posed by security vulnerabilities associated with the asset	80%
Percentage of risk remaining after mitigation/prevention steps are deployed	5%

If we replace the factors in the equation with these values, the calculation becomes

$$100\% \times 80\% \times 5\%,$$

which results in the risk percentage being 4%.

Calculating Risk from Multiple Vulnerabilities for Any Asset

In the typical case where multiple threats are posed to an asset, the total risk for all the threats is calculated by adding up the sum of all risks. Because this calculation is designed to give an overall impression of the risk faced by an asset, the idea is not to calculate an actual value but to look at the relative values across all assets in scope. It is easy to understand the reasoning here: as several risk factors for any one asset could total over 100%, it is the relative values that are important here.

This step is, of course, optional. It utilizes the risk calculations generated from the previous calculations of risk for each vulnerability. The total risk is calculated as follows:

total % risk = sum of all the individual risks for each vulnerability, or
vulnerability A + vulnerability B + vulnerability C

Factors for calculating $ value at risk	% values assigned by the security technology team
Risk for vulnerability A	4%
Risk for vulnerability B	10%
Risk for vulnerability C	17%

If we replace the factors with their values, the calculation becomes

4% + 10% + 17% = 31% total risk

Calculating the Monetary Value at Risk for Any Asset

So far, we have just calculated pure risk for each asset. The next step is to add, for any key asset in question, the estimated monetary loss expected as the result of a breach.

For simplicity, the currency in the following example is in dollars. Here, the dollar value at risk, $1,000,000, is multiplied by the risk value previously calculated, 4%.

The value at risk might have been obtained using the executive straw poll in Chapter 8 for determining estimated values at risk from security breaches.

The calculation for monetary value at risk is

$ value at risk = $ value of the expected loss for a specific asset
× total % risk facing the asset

Factors for calculating $ value at risk	Value of factors
$ value of expected loss for a specific asset	$1,000,000
Total % risk facing the asset	4%

Replacing the factors with their values, the calculation becomes

$$\$1,000,000 \times 4\% = \$40,000 \text{ at risk}$$

The value of the risk calculations shows executives the relative risk of various threat/vulnerability/mitigation groupings.

The monetary value at risk for any asset gives executives a basis for comparing potential losses across various key assets. We will see in Chapter 8 how the value at risk is used in the calculation of return on information security investment.

These calculations are available for your use in spreadsheet format in the downloads for this book.

Sources of Web Application Security Vulnerability Information

The severity of many vulnerabilities is well documented and publicly available. Several of the most useful resources for finding this information are

- **Open Web Application Security Project (OWASP):** (www.owasp.org) Based on information sent to the organization from security experts around the world, this site publishes lists of the most severe web application vulnerabilities.

- **National Vulnerability Database (NVD):** (http://nvd.nist.gov/) Sponsored by the National Institute of Standards and Technology, this vulnerability resource focuses on servers and networks. Its Common Vulnerability Scoring System (CVSS) provides an open framework for communicating the characteristics and impacts of IT vulnerabilities.

- **US Computer Emergency Readiness Team (US CERT):** (www.us-cert.gov) This site is maintained by the National Homeland Security's team that leads the cybersecurity efforts in United States .

- **Web Application Security Consortium (WASC):** (www.webappsec.org/) This site is run by WASC, a not-for-profit organization made up of an international group of experts, industry practitioners, and organizational representatives who produce open-source and widely agreed-upon best-practice security standards for the World Wide Web.

Summary

It is important for executives to understand the relationship between their key assets and the risk and threats to those assets early on in the risk analysis process. To do this, they must understand the meaning of risk, relative risk, threats, vulnerabilities, breach, compromise, remediation, and countermeasures in the context of IT security. Management needs a simple mechanism for estimating the monetary value of an asset's potential losses that result from a security breach. I describe an executive straw poll method for doing so in Chapter 8.

In the next chapter, we will look at vulnerabilities and their risk severity, which can be directly fed into the risk analysis calculations we generated in this chapter.

■ ■ ■

CHAPTER 2

Types of Web Application Security Testing

The purpose of web application security testing is to find any security weaknesses or vulnerabilities within an application and its environment, to document the vulnerabilities, and to explain how to fix or remediate them. The business drivers behind the testing may be requirements of corporate policy, security requirements mandated by the corporate financial auditors or an internal audit department, compliance requirements for PCI or other industry standards, or compliance with regulatory standards such as Sarbanes-Oxley or HIPAA. An evidentiary type of audit report, which contains evidence to back up claims of vulnerabilities, is even better, as the report will stand the test of time, and, over the years, explanations and thoughts about how the vulnerabilities were found may fade from people's memories.

There are several types of testing methodologies. These include web application security audits, vulnerability assessments, and penetration tests. These methodologies have different scopes and goals, each with strengths and weaknesses. For clarity, these methodologies are all different from one another, but vulnerability testing and penetration testing may also both be part of an overall audit. However, an audit may contain steps that are not related to either vulnerability testing or penetration testing, as described in the section "Web Application Audits."

The testing methodologies, in turn, can be executed with different levels of automation. Some testing is done in a completely automated fashion and other testing is done with a high component of manual intervention. This chapter briefly describes the goals and differences of the various types of testing and audits but does not attempt to delve into details of audit methodologies or audit standards to which audits may adhere.

Once testing is complete, the next recommended step is to fix the vulnerabilities identified by the testing. Once remediation is complete, the step following that should be postremediation testing to ensure all the repairs were done successfully.

In Chapter 3, we will walk through the process of these steps and describe in detail common web application vulnerabilities that are found during the course of audits, vulnerability testing, and penetration testing.

Understanding the Testing Process

Web application security testing comes in all shapes and sizes and it is sometimes difficult to differentiate between them. To add to the confusion, the names of the tests are sometimes used interchangeably, which sets incorrect expectations of all the tests concerned.

In a nutshell, the different aspects of web application testing can be understood in terms of the questions they answer:

- A web application audit answers the question, Is an organization implementing its web application policies correctly?

- A vulnerability assessment answers the question, What security weaknesses or vulnerabilities exist within an application?

- A penetration test answers the question, Was the tester, in a given amount of time, able to compromise any of the vulnerabilities?

- Postremediation testing answers the question, Have the vulnerabilities found during testing been completely remediated?

To summarize the terms used here since they seem very similar, an *audit* has the greatest scope and includes vulnerability testing, and *web app audits* try to find vulnerabilities in a broader scope of subjects including policies and procedures. *Vulnerability testing* is usually passive and seeks to identify but not compromise the vulnerabilities it identifies. *Penetration testing* is the next possible step after identifying the vulnerabilities and attempts to compromise those vulnerabilities. Another way of saying the same thing is that whereas vulnerability testing just identifies technical vulnerabilities, penetration testing actually tries to exploit those vulnerabilities. *Postremediation testing* occurs after remediation and identifies the degree of remediation success.

The main reason penetration testing is done is to satisfy a specific governmental or very high security requirement. However, in some cases companies simply want proof that the systems can be compromised. I recommend using the funds that would otherwise be used for penetration testing for postremediation testing and for implementing ongoing, regular vulnerability testing.

Web Application Audits

The scope of an audit is generally a superset of a vulnerability assessment. The scope may include other software associated with the application, such as databases, access controls for the application environment, application documentation, security policies and procedures for managing the application and its environment, change management, revision management, backup and restore procedures, and so on.

The audit process starts with a specific, clearly defined scope of requirements. These requirements may include vulnerability testing for the application and its associated database, access controls, and security policies and procedures.

The first step of the audit involves a planning meeting to ensure all objectives will be met by the various planned audit activities. Activities include collecting data about the security posture of the environment through vulnerability and other technological-security testing, manual security testing, interviews with staff members, and a review of operational and security-related policy/procedures documentation. After the data-collection phase of the audit is completed, analysis is done on all the data collected in order to create the required deliverables of:

1. Any available evidence of the presence of vulnerabilities

2. A description of the vulnerabilities

3. Recommended remediation for each type of vulnerability

4. Each vulnerability's levels of security risk and business risk.

5. An executive summary that translates all the technical jargon into business risks upon which financial decision makers can act.

Vulnerability Assessment

A vulnerability assessment is a subset of an audit and is focused on finding weaknesses or vulnerabilities within the web application. It involves real-time testing and exercises the application components such as all input fields. There are different vulnerability testing tools commercially available such as Nexpose, Nessus, and NMap.

Vulnerability assessments can be completely automated or have a manual component. A manual component is usually done by an expert tester who utilizes several testing tools over a predetermined scope of time to find vulnerabilities in a step-by-step manner. The steps may involve launching several tools, with the intention that a vulnerability missed by one tool will be identified by another.

The steps may also involve the tester diving deeper into any vulnerability that she thinks may lead to finding other vulnerabilities. For instance, if a tester finds weak encryption in one section of a transaction processing application, she may dive more deeply into that section to look for weaknesses relating to out-of-date security certificates.

There are upsides and downsides to both fully automated vulnerability testing and for manual testing.

Fully Automated Testing

Fully automated testing is done using tools that are designed to run autonomously once they are given target IP addresses and URLs to test. Prior to starting the automated testing, the tester first needs to make sure the targets have visibility. For instance, if the IP addresses and URLs that are in scope for testing reside behind a firewall, the security person responsible for these items needs to grant him secure-access.

High-quality automated testing tools should have access to back-end databases of both current vulnerabilities and current threats so that they can test comprehensively and then tune out false positives. The method for tuning out false positives is to compare the vulnerabilities against the list of threats and then eliminate reporting on vulnerabilities for which there are no corresponding threats.

The main benefits of automated testing include the following:

- **100 percent scope:** These tests run very fast and the scope of testing is 100 percent of an application.

- **Exact number of instances reported:** Since the test scope is 100 percent of an application, the tool can enumerate the exact number of instances of each type of vulnerability.

- **Cost effectiveness:** These tests are less expensive to run than ones involving expert testers' time. For instance, an automated test may take one person-day to implement and only minutes to run. A comparable manual test would take four person-days to execute. If the testing tool can be rented or used as part of an outsourced service, then the all-in costs of the automated testing tool may be significantly less than for manual testing.

- **Timely actionable information:** Since the tests are less expensive than manual ones, it is more affordable to run them often, such as monthly, to obtain timely information about newly evolving vulnerabilities.

The primary downside of automated tests is that they cannot find all of the types of vulnerabilities. For example, the testing algorithms cannot anticipate issues that arise with real-time data, such as work flow errors or weak password protection.

Manual Testing

If manual testing is done by an expert in web application security, then this methodology offers the greatest-possible depth of testing. Manual testing is a step-by-step process where the tester looks for vulnerabilities, and, when they are found, attempts to drill down further into the vulnerabilities to clarify their magnitude and just how risky they are.

A manual tester uses testing tools to conduct much of the testing but directs the course of the tools. Also, since every tool has its limitations, a skilled tester will use at least two tools in order to minimize the chances of missing a vulnerability.

Since manual testing always has time and cost limitations, it is done only on sample sections of a web application. The reports then identify where and what type of vulnerabilities were found. Recommendations for where remediation can be done in every instance of the security weakness.

The most significant benefit of manual testing is that it can be more granular than automated testing and cover a wider scope. Since human experts are conducting the testing, they can understand vulnerabilities that automated testing tools cannot parse or understand. Also, experienced testers can dive deeper in an iterative manner to explore suspicious circumstances.

However, there are several downsides to manual testing:

- **Expense**: Person power is expensive.

- **Scope limited to sampling**: Since every testing engagement has a finite amount of time allocated for expert testers' time, the testing is often limited to a sample of the application.

- **Number of instances not reported**: The total number of instances of each vulnerability is not usually reported. Instead, the type of vulnerabilities is reported, and it is up to the web application owner to identify all the instances.

Combining Automated and Manual Testing

The most accurate determinant of vulnerabilities and risk is the use of automated testing in concert with manual testing. Automated testing can be done monthly to provide information on a regular, timely basis at a relatively low cost. Manual testing can be done periodically, such as on a quarterly or annual basis, to find the vulnerabilities not detectable by the automated tester at a relatively higher cost.

The optimization of lower-cost automated testing in conjunction with higher-cost manual testing provides the benefits of both worlds:

- 100 percent scope of the application is tested

- Regular, timely reports of the latest vulnerabilities

- Quarterly or annual deeper-dive testing to identify vulnerabilities not otherwise found

A valuable enhancement to identifying vulnerabilities is to proceed to map the vulnerabilities *against a database of existing exploits and attacks "in the wild"* and then allocate higher risks to those vulnerabilities for which there exist actual threats.

Penetration Testing

A penetration test is a deeper dive of a vulnerability test. Here, the expert tester attempts to compromise vulnerabilities he finds. The tester's goal it to prove he can gain a high level of administrative access. Testing is often done by teams of one or more testers, called tiger teams.

The main benefit of a penetration test is the proof of the risk. A compromised vulnerability proves the degree of risk. On the other hand, the time it takes for penetration testing is expensive, and it does not reduce risk; it only verifies the risk.

I believe it is a better return on investment for most companies to spend their security funds on eliminating vulnerabilities and hardening their security infrastructure rather than testing vulnerabilities that they already know need to be mitigated.

Postremediation Testing

It is surprising that vulnerabilities are sometimes not remediated even after a comprehensive web application test. Yet this problem often occurs and for many reasons. Sometimes remediations are effectively implemented but then unwound by an additional development of the application. Sometimes technologists remediate some but not all the instances of every type of vulnerability. There are also instances where third-party operators inadvertently undo the benefits of remediation by operational changes they make.

Therefore, a postremedial audit is a very useful tool for ensuring the remediation plan was successfully executed. The postremedial audit is usually smaller in scope than the initial audit and its focus is on identifying whether or not the remediation recommendations in the initial audit have been done correctly. The remediation audit report is therefore comprised of yes-or-no responses for each vulnerability in regard to whether each vulnerability has been successfully remediated.

Important Report Deliverables for All Testing Reports

Reports are the last stage of an audit engagement and are done after the testing team has completed information gathering, done the requisite analysis, drawn conclusions, and made recommendations. If the report is not crystal clear, actionable, complete, and easy to read, and does not include a provision for the recipient to ask questions, then the report may have little value. I have seen reports that were filled with unanalyzed data, did not provide actionable remediations, did not differentiate the levels of risk of the vulnerabilities, did not transparently identify evidence of vulnerabilities, did not explain what tools and methodologies were used, did not organize the results data in a format that is clear and able to be easily referenced, and did not have provisions for any subsequent questions to be answered.

Readers of audit reports want to see crystal clear observations, specific remedial recommendations, brevity that does not impune accuracy, and a linkage between vulnerabilities and their related business risks. That is what a good audit report provides.

Testing reports are most useful when they:

- provide only actionable data. This means filtering out false positives.

- provide up-to-date and accurate analysis based on extensive and constantly updated databases of vulnerabilities, malware, and attacks that exist in the wild.

- report the technical information by correlating each vulnerability with its:

  - associated threat

  - risk of compromise

  - business risk

- remediation

- evidence of existence

- number of occurrences by vulnerability type wherever possible

- report estimated time for remediation for each type of vulnerability.

- identify the tools and methodology used for testing.

- precisely identify the scope of the audit, including IP address ranges, URLs, number of employees interviewed, number of pages of documentation read, the dates during which testing was done, and so forth.

- publish a Q & A session for recipients postreport with full transparency and disclosure for all types of questions.

This is a general list that will vary for reports looking at specific types of testing, such as penetration testing, where the vulnerabilities may already be known and the focus is on whether or not they can be compromised by a testing team of a specific size and testing for a specific period of time. The report for a postremedial audit will be severely truncated and can be as simple as a column of yes-or-no observations added to the vulnerability list in the initial audit portion.

Summary

There is a wide range of types and methodologies of web application security testing. It is important for those with expectations of the results of testing to understand the differences and overlap between different types of tests and how they are performed. This is important in order to ensure that expectations of results are clearly understood before funds are spent on the actual testing.

There is a different return on investment for each type of testing. Some testing is more drill down in depth, such as penetration testing, but may not have any return on investment at all. Other testing, such as automated regular-vulnerability testing, will be relatively inexpensive but may have a huge return on investment and may also meet all the business requirements imposed upon those responsible for web application security. In between these extremes exist various degrees and subsets of web application audits, whose return on investments will vary with the business requirements that drive the underlying testing needs.

The testing process (defining the pieces) for web application security audits, vulnerability assessments, and penetration testing can vary and is generally divided between automated and manual testing. Testing can have various degrees of automation and manual testing. Generally, automated testing is faster and less expensive than manual testing. There is a variety of testing tools available for web application security testing. It is useful to test with at least two tools to improve the chances that any vulnerability that is not found by one tool will be identified by another. Manual testing can find vulnerabilities that fully automated testing simply cannot.

After testing is completed, remediation should be done to fix vulnerabilities found during the testing phase. Postremediation testing should be done to make sure remediation has been done successfully. It is very important that false positives are tuned out during the analysis phase of all testing. This ensures that the reports are as meaningful and as actionable as possible.

Test reports must be clear, complete, actionable, and accompanied by an opportunity for the recipient to ask questions about the information provided.

■ ■ ■

CHAPTER 3

Web Application Vulnerabilities and the Damage They Can Cause

The obvious risks to a security breach are that unauthorized individuals: 1) can gain access to restricted information and 2) may be able to escalate their privileges in order to compromise the application and the entire application environment. The areas that can be compromised include user and system administration accounts.

This chapter identifies the major classes of web application vulnerabilities, gives some examples of actual vulnerabilities found in real-life web application audits, and describes their associated level of risk. The classes are:

- authentication
- session management
- access control
- input validation
- redirects and forwards
- injection flaws
- unauthorized view of data
- error handling
- cross-site scripting
- security misconfigurations
- denial of service
- related security issues

Chapter 4 provides remediation guidance for each of the vulnerability classes and specific vulnerabilities described in this chapter. The vulnerability and remediation information also is provided in a consolidated spreadsheet that you can sort or add to is available with the downloads for this book. (See the Source Code/Downloads tab on the book's Apress product page: www.apress.com/9781484201497.)

IT-security and web-application-security auditors including myself have seen more than our fill of real-life vulnerabilities. I am sharing some of these examples in this book to make the information as relevant as possible to the reader.

Lack of Sufficient Authentication

Risk level: **HIGH**

Correctly checking authentication credentials and then providing access to a web application accordingly are paramount operations for a server to perform when providing security and privacy.

Prior to accessing a web application, a server should require end users to authenticate themselves and confirm they are in fact who they purport to be.

In addition, strong authentication using valid credentials is the first security checkpoint for protecting web applications. One of the biggest web application weaknesses is the failure to provide a means of strong authentication.

The obvious risk to an authentication breach is that an unauthorized individual or computer program can gain access to restricted information and may be able to escalate their privileges in order to compromise an application and the entire application environment.

The compromised applications can, of course, include user and system-administration accounts. Additionally, the individual could gain unauthorized access to the targeted account, to another user's account, and/or have the opportunity to view sensitive or private information.

Weak Password Controls

Risk level: **HIGH**

Passwords are one of the most important elements to Internet security. They must be protected and changed regularly because an attacker or malicious user can mount a password-guessing attack (e.g., through brute force or a dictionary) that can have a high probability of success. Once a password has been guessed, the attacker can then log on to the application using the "guessed" account credentials and operate on the user's behalf (e.g., change the user's profile, mount attacks using fields available only to authenticated users, access sensitive information).

As auditors, we often find a situation like this wherein the user policy did not require users to have a complex password (such as a combination of alphanumeric characters, use of lower- and upper-case characters, etc.). One of the auditors was able to breach this weak security and gain access to the account with a simple password ("abcde").

Passwords Submitted Without Encryption

Risk level: **HIGH**

Passwords submitted over an unencrypted connection are vulnerable to capture by an attacker that is suitably positioned on the network to monitor and capture traffic. This includes any malicious party located on the user's own network, within her ISP, within the ISP used by the application, and within the application's hosting infrastructure, as well as networks along the communications path.

A real-life example that I've seen is credentials being sent in clear text on an unencrypted communications channel that was susceptible to eavesdropping. *Unencrypted* means the opposite of *encrypted*. Encryption is the conversion of data into a form that an unauthorized reader cannot easily interpret. An authorized reader then converts encrypted data back into its original form so it can be understood using a method of decryption. There are many methods for encryption/decryption that are called algorithms in the security world. An algorithm can be as simple as Morse code or as complex as those used for military purposes.

Username Harvesting

Risk level: **HIGH**

Usernames need to be protected and never shared, as they can be used to try to obtain unauthorized access to an account.

Like passwords, usernames are susceptible to being harvested with a brute-force method or by simply finding the e-mail address associated with them by doing research on the Internet. An attacker or a malicious user can leverage these items as a potential vulnerability with which to gather information. That person can then guess usernames in the login screen, which will return a detailed error message if the account does not exist. This information can in turn be used to devise more precise attacks (e.g., password guessing for valid accounts only, focusing on reducing the number of hacking attempts to a level that may not be detected by any automated methods).

Login screens are also configured to display detailed error messages that reveal username information, and in a worst-case scenario, this information can also be exploited to gather information.

Weak Session Management

Risk level: **LOW-HIGH**

Session management is something that most users are unaware of, but this is an essential security methodology for foiling hackers from attempting to break into and take control of a session. The idea is for a server to be able to regularly verify that the user conducting the interaction or conversation is the one the server thinks it is.

If an application doesn't use transport-level encryption (SSL or TLS) to protect all sensitive communications passing between a client and a server, the communications between them is more highly susceptible to a security breach. Communications are intended to include the login mechanism and related functions where sensitive data can be accessed and where privileged actions are performed.

Secure Sockets Layer (SSL) is a standard security technology, or protocol, for establishing an encrypted link between a web server ("server") and a web browser ("client"). SSL uses encryption technology to secure both the communications link (referred to as a tunnel) and the data being transmitted.

SSL has been superseded by a more advanced technology called Transport Layer Security (TLS). TLS relies on third-party or self-signed certificates to create keys that are used for encryption. TLS is the successor of SSL. TLS is more secure than its predecessor. However, SSL is more widely used than TLS.

We found many real-life examples where web applications are not correctly establishing session encryption. Since HTTP does not provide this capability, it is up to the web applications to provide it. HTTP is short for hypertext transfer protocol, which is the underlying protocol used by the World Wide Web. HTTP defines how messages are formatted and transmitted and what actions web servers and browsers should take in response to various commands.

During the course of two separate audits, we could not determine the level of SSL security because we could not explicitly determine whether the SSL keys were verified by hashing or if they were simply encrypted while stored. Since interviews were not in the scope of these particular audits, there was no way for an auditor to verify the facts. If the SSL keys were simply encrypted but not hashed, then they would be susceptible to compromise if an attacker could decode the encryption. In addition, during the course of these two audits, there was no evidence of salting being used in this environment, which was another indication that hashing was not used in these environments.

Hashing is a form of one-way encryption. The idea is to protect critical information such as passwords by never having to store them, something that allows them to be compromised. By hashing them and storing the hashed value instead of storing the actual critical information, the risk to the critical information is reduced. The recipient must recreate the hashing process and compare hashed values to make sure the critical information is correct. *Salting* is additional protection for hashing. Salting is adding random extra information into the critical data before it is hashed. This process makes it more difficult for a person of malintent to guess critical information.

For the purposes of this book, a session is the activity carried on between a web browser and a web server from the time of logon to the time of logout. It is conducted over the HTTP or HTTPS protocols. In the bigger picture, a session is really a TCP or UDP session that deals with any protocol and doesn't necessarily directly relate to HTTP or HTTPS, although in the context of web application security it can.

Transmission control protocol (TCP) is one of the most basic of the group of protocols that makes the Internet function. TCP allows for requests and responses, and a TCP request is simply a request for service. User datagram protocol (UDP) is a simplified version of a transmission protocol that provides for limited messaging to be exchanged between computers in a network that uses the internet protocol (IP). It does not provide as comprehensive a function as the TCP protocol.

Weak SSL Ciphers Support

Risk level: **HIGH**

A standard method of securing communications between a user and a web application is the use of encryption. If the method of encryption is outdated or weak, then the security is weak.

There are too many examples we have seen during the audit process where a remote service supports the use of weak SSL ciphers. An attacker could break the weak cipher's encryption and perform a "man-in-the-middle" attack to eavesdrop on a user's session. As previously mentioned, SSL is a standard security technology or protocol for establishing an encrypted link between a server and a client. SSL uses encryption technology to secure both the communications link (referred to as a tunnel) and the data being transmitted. The cipher for SSL is the encryption methodology that a particular version of SSL is using. SSL can utilize a variety of ciphers, some of which are more secure than others.

Information Submitted Using the GET Method

Risk level: **MEDIUM**

There are several methods that HTTP utilizes to make requests for information, including GET and POST. Since HTTP is unencrypted, it is important for web application programmers to consider the security weaknesses inherent in its use of the GET method, making GET a poor choice for transmitting sensitive data such as user names and passwords. Not to drill in too deeply, but it is the clear-text nature of the HTTP protocol that makes it insecure. GET displays data in clear text in the URL, and the URL can in turn be seen in server logs, in client browser histories, and in any forward or reverse proxy servers between a user and a web application server. This makes sensitive data retrievable for unauthorized persons.

URL request strings may also be displayed onscreen, bookmarked, or e-mailed around by users. They may be disclosed to third parties via the HTTP referrer header when any off-site links are followed. The HTTP referrer header is a data field, such as a hyperlink on a web site, that drives visits to another web site. Examples of HTTP referrers are other web sites, search engines, link lists, e-mails, and banner advertisements.

Here again, we see many client web applications that use the GET method to submit sensitive information, such as session ID (session token) and passwords, which are transmitted within the query string of the requested URL.

Self-Signed Certificates, Insecure Keys, and Passwords

Risk level: **HIGH**

Certificates, keys, and passwords are fundamental to Internet security. The most reliable certificates are managed by third-party certificate authorities. Self-signed and self-managed versions are not as trustworthy. They are good cover for an imposter posing as a valid organization, and the SSL or TLS *man-in-the-middle* attack often uses self-signed certificates to eavesdrop on SSL or TLS connections. A man-in-the-middle attack is done by an eavesdropper of a communication session that subsequently inserts itself into the session and tricks the parties at either end to think they are still communicating directly with each other. In fact, they are both communicating with the man in the middle. This attack succeeds when the attacker impersonates each endpoint to the satisfaction of the other.

On another note, users should be wary of the warning statements about invalid certificates, which indicate that a self-signed certificate has no outside validation.

We saw a situation where a server's X.509 certificates were indeed self-signed, suggesting that they were not obtained from a certificate authority. If the certificates were susceptible to being viewed by an unauthorized party, then that party could create bogus certificates and attempt to hijack a session.

Username Harvesting Applied to Forgotten Password Process

Risk level: **HIGH**

A relatively simple way for hackers to gain unauthorized access to usernames is via a password recovery process. We have frequently seen registered users' information being revealed. This happens through the unnecessary display of user identification in a password error message. An attacker or malicious user can leverage this vulnerability to gather information on registered users. This information will assist in devising more precise attacks (e.g., password guessing focusing on valid accounts only to reduce the number of attempts, at a level that may not be detected by automated monitoring).

Autocomplete Enabled on Password Fields

Risk level: **LOW**

Another relatively easy way for hackers to gain unauthorized access to usernames is to see them displayed in autocomplete as soon as the first part of the name is typed.

The web application contains HTML form fields that contain an input password when Autocomplete is not set to Off. Passwords stored on connecting client machines could expose user accounts to malicious third parties.

Most browsers have a facility to remember user credentials that are entered into HTML forms. This function can be configured by the user and also by applications that employ user credentials. If the function is enabled, credentials entered by users are stored on their local computer and retrieved by the browser on future visits to the same application.

The stored credentials can be captured by an attacker who gains access to the client computer, either locally or through a remote compromise. Further, methods exist whereby a malicious web site can retrieve the stored credentials for other applications by exploiting browser vulnerabilities or through application-level cross-domain attacks.

While storing information on a web application does not represent a risk in and of itself, it does mean that users who use the affected forms may have their credentials saved in their browsers, which could in turn lead to a loss of confidential information if a shared host is used or their machine is compromised.

Session IDs Nonrandom and Too Short

Risk level: **MEDIUM**

Since it is a security weakness to use unique session identifiers that are easy to guess, they should be as random and as long as possible.

A Session ID or session identifier or session token is an identification device used to identify a user to a web application. The web application creates session tokens and sends them to a user's browser. The web browser in turn sends the token back to the web application along with any requests or information in order to identify the user.

An attacker could guess token values for authenticated users, which could lead to unauthorized access in the form of session hijacking. From the point of hijacking onward, any action performed by a malicious user will then be logged as being performed by the legitimate user.

Weak Access Control

Risk level: **LOW-HIGH**

Restricting or controlling access to an application, or for that matter to all important processes and files, is the most important aspect of security. A prime goal of hackers is to gain unauthorized access to applications and then increase the priority level of their access privileges.

In general, strict authentication should be enforced at both the application and server levels in order to minimize the chance of unauthorized access to confidential information. This process is prone to administrative errors particularly if it is not kept simple and implemented in a way that is easy to test.

During a particular audit, we identified that access control to a specific page was not enforced either at the application or server level, which may have allowed an attacker to impersonate an authorized user and gain access to confidential information.Specifically, the URL pointing to subsections of the application was allowed to be changed by the user without further authentication.

During the interview portion of the audit, the auditor further discovered that some of the authentication process code was written in-house as part of the client-side application in order to communicate with the third-party authentication engine. This nonunified code was hard to administer and prone to errors.

Frameable Response (Clickjacking)

Risk level: **LOW**

If IFrames are used in an application without any restriction on the source of the content, then a clickjacking attack can occur. An attacker can do this by embedding an IFrame on any web site and overlaying the invisible IFrame on top of legitimate content. When a user clicks a legitimate-looking button, the attacker's button or link is actually being clicked.

By inducing users to then perform actions such as mouse clicks and keystrokes, the attacker can cause them to unwittingly carry out harmful actions. This can result in a user's computer being hijacked and confidential data getting compromised. IFrames are tools available to web site developers that allow them to divide a screen into different sections. This enables each section to get information from its own separate information source.

What makes this a very powerful way of attacking is that it is actually done within the bounds of the HTML specification, which means that the web site is working as expected. The attackers just exploit this feature for malicious attacks. Therefore, web site administrators may not know that something is wrong until complaints come in from users. It is hard to pinpoint that an attack has taken place because everything on the site looks the same and the clickjack element has been thoroughly disguised as harmless.

Cached HTTPS Response

Risk level: **MEDIUM**

Cached HTTPS responses are caused by sensitive information from application responses being stored in the local cache memory of a user's workstation. This information may be viewed and retrieved by other parties who have access to the same computer simply by looking at the cache. This situation is exacerbated if a laptop is stolen or if a user accesses the web application from a public terminal.

Cache refers to copies of recently viewed web pages and associated data that are stored on a local disk. This local data improves web application access speed but it is also easy for anyone to find. For instance, Microsoft Internet Explorer cache files can be easily found in the Users File and labeled as Cache or Temporary Internet Files. In some browsers including Internet Explorer, cache content may be created by both HTTP and HTTPS.

An example of this vulnerability appeared while conducting a test during a valid user session, where a user's browser did store content received from the web application in cache.

Sensitive Information Disclosed in HTML Comments

Risk level: **LOW**

Many web application programmers use HTML comments to help debug the application. While adding descriptive comments can be very useful for developers to explain things to others and to remind themselves about how program code works, they should never be able to be viewed by users, who might be potential hackers. To worsen the situation, some programmers also leave sensitive data in comments. By sensitive data, I am referring to things like file names that are related to the web application, old links or links that were not meant to be browsed by users, and old code fragments. An attacker who finds this type of data in comments can map the application's structure and files, expose hidden parts of the site, and study the fragments of code to reverse engineer the application. These are stepping stones from which an attacker may develop a damaging attack against the site.

HTTP Server Type and Version Number Disclosed

Risk level: **LOW**

It is always good security practice to not reveal any information about the manufacturer or version of any network hardware or software since this information can be used by a hacker to further investigate vulnerabilities associated with that specific technology.

For instance, a common audit observation is that HTTP headers in HTTP responses from web servers disclose the web server type and version number. An attacker or a malicious user could exploit this information to mount attacks against the known vulnerabilities associated with the type and version of the web server. These attacks may compromise the remote system and allow the attacker to obtain administrator-level permissions on the web server, which will grant full access to the system and all the data stored on it.

The remote system can then be leveraged to execute additional attacks against internal systems in the organization.

Insufficient Session Expiration

Risk level: **MEDIUM**

I previously discussed the importance of secure sessions. It is also important that sessions are changed frequently to make hacking them more difficult. Insufficient session expiration may permit an attacker to reuse old session credentials or session IDs for authorization. One auditor was able to replay a single request to the web application after logging out. A session is the activity carried on between a web browser and a web server from the time of logon to the time of logout. It runs over the HTTP or HTTPS protocols.

The lack of proper session expiration may also improve the likelihood of success of certain attacks. An attacker may intercept a session ID, possibly via a network sniffer or cross-site scripting attack. In another scenario, a user might access a web site from a shared computer (such as at a library, Internet cafe, or open work environment). Insufficient session expiration could allow an attacker to use the browser's back button to access web pages previously accessed by the victim.

HTML Does Not Specify Charset

Risk level: **LOW**

An easy-to-overlook security problem with creating HTML content is the developer being able to specify which character set he wants to use; it is best default practice to use the most secure one.

If a web response states that it contains HTML content but does not specify a character set, then the browser may analyze the HTML and attempt to determine which character set it appears to be using. HTML is an Internet standard that specifies how web pages are formatted and displayed.

Even if the majority of the HTML actually employs a standard character set such as UTF-8, the presence of nonstandard characters anywhere in the response may cause the browser to interpret the content using a different character set.

This can have unexpected results and can lead to cross-site scripting vulnerabilities in which nonstandard encodings like UTF-7 can be used to bypass the application's defensive filters. In most cases, the absence of a charset directive does not constitute a security flaw, particularly if the response contains static content. Always review the contents of the response and the context in which it appears to determine whether any vulnerability exists.

Session Fixation

Risk level: **HIGH**

Yet another issue with the security of sessions occurs when sessions are not fully terminated when the activity related to that session is ended. Many web application audits have revealed that there exists a serious cookie problem where the web application authenticates a user without first invalidating the existing session. The result is that the application continues to use the session associated with the previous user. This creates a risk of users gaining access to data that they do not have authorization to view.

Insecure Cookies

Risk level: **MEDIUM**

Since cookies can be part of access controls, five common security flaws related to them are aptly included here at the end of the access control section. An HTTP cookie is a short file of information sent by a web server to a web browser. The message is then sent back to the server each time the browser requests a page from it. The purpose of the use of the cookie is to enhance the user's experience with the web application by directing the user to the information of most interest within it.

We often see that the session tokens are not properly protected where the web application environment provides a session capability; for example, when the user's session ID is displayed in the URL. This creates a vulnerability where an attacker could hijack an active session and assume the identity of a valid user.

Even if authentication is required, it may be possible for a user to conduct it using legitimate credentials but then change the session ID in the URL line to access another user's data without requiring reauthentication. A session token, or session identifier or session ID, is an identification device used to identify a user to a web application. The web application creates session tokens and sends them to a user's browser. The web browser in turn sends the token back to the web application along with any requests or information in order to identify the user.

An external or even internal attacker could leverage the flaws in the authentication or session management functions (e.g., exposed accounts, passwords, session IDs) to impersonate users and even to escalate their privileges.

As a general comment, developers frequently build custom authentication and session management schemes, but building these correctly is difficult. As a result, custom schemes frequently have flaws in areas such as the login/logout, password management, time-outs, Remember Me buttons, secret question, account updates, and so forth. Finding such flaws can sometimes be difficult, as each implementation is unique.

Cookies with No Secure Flag

Risk level: **MEDIUM**

A cookie with no secure flag is another example of when it is important to not unnecessarily reveal details even of a cookie. As a reminder, a cookie is a short file of information sent from a server to a browser and its contents should remain unavailable to potential hackers.

If the secure flag is set on a cookie, browsers will not submit the cookie in any requests that use an unencrypted HTTP connection, thereby preventing the cookie from being intercepted by an attacker monitoring network traffic. If the secure flag is not set on the cookie, the cookie will be transmitted in clear text.

Cookies Set to Expire in the Distant Future

Risk level: **MEDIUM**

Prolonged expiration is another example of problems that can arise with secure cookies. It is important to make sure that cookies do not last too long in order to reduce the chances of them being read by a party with malicious intent.

A user's session can be used by anyone with knowledge of the cookie. Since cookies are not necessarily destroyed upon tabbing to a new page or to closing a window, it can be easy for anyone with physical access to the user's computer to reuse an existing session.

We once saw a case where the configuration for cookie expiration was set for 30 years from its initial creation, where best practices suggest cookie expiration should be only as long as required for its useful life, pending any legal requirements for longevity.

Cookies with No HttpOnly Flag

Risk level: **LOW**

HttpOnly cookies are created by a server application and have security value. They cannot be read from or written to in JavaScript on the client side, with these possibilities only existing on the server side.

If the HttpOnly flag is not set or the cookie is created in client-side JavaScript, the cookie can be read from and written to in client-side JavaScript as well as on the server side. This is not desirable from a security perspective.

Client-side malicious code, such as a malicious JavaScript, could read the cookie content. An attacker could leverage this vulnerability and capture confidential cookies via an injected script. This confidential data can be used to build an attack.

Cookies Created on the Client Side

Risk level: **LOW**

The same concern as for cookies where the HttpOnly flag is not set, a party other than the trusted server can send potentially malicious data back to the server within a cookie.

Malicious client-side code could be used to manipulate a site's cookies. This makes it possible to move the enforcement of cookie logic from the application server to the client-side application browser. It could allow an attacker to send unauthorized cookies with malicious intent.

Cookies Scoped to a Parent Domain

Risk level: **LOW**

Another layer of security for cookies involves restricting their access to only the applications with which they are intended to interact.

A cookie's domain attribute determines which domains can access the cookie. Browsers will automatically submit the cookie in requests to in-scope domains, which will also be able to access the cookie. If a cookie is scoped to a parent domain, then that cookie will be accessible to the parent domain and also by any of its other subdomains.

If the cookie contains sensitive data (such as a session token) and is accessible to subdomains, then unauthorized persons could possibly gain access to the confidential information contained in the cookies. A *subdomain* is a child or member of a main domain. The main domain is called the *root*. For example, a root domain may be named abcd.com and a subdomain may be called childof.abc.com.

Weak Input Validation at the Application Level

Risk level: **HIGH**

Unauthorized access is the golden nugget for hackers, and strong protection against unauthorized access is strong validation of the identities of users requesting access to an application.

While it is common practice for web applications to verify access rights before making functionality visible in the user interface (UI), it should also be common practice to revalidate authentication at various important access points within an application.

If revalidation of the user ID and user requests are not verified, an attacker may be able to forge requests within an existing session in order to access unauthorized or privileged information.

For example, in a transaction-processing web application, a user may be required to first authenticate just for the privilege of gaining access to the application; a second time when she selects the transaction class she wishes to execute, such as buy, sell, trade, or look-up; and a third time to manage the movement of currency.

Lack of Validated Input Allowing Automatic Script Execution

Risk level: **HIGH**

All user input must be filtered to restrict any data not expected and wanted by an application. This includes any strings or groups of characters, especially control characters, which can be used to gain unauthorized privileges and control of the environment.

We have found quite the opposite to exist in real-world situations, where user input, such as messages, text, and data input into e-mail fields, was not validated or filtered before being accepted. This insecure manner of operation fails to prevent a malicious user from inserting malicious code into the input fields. An attacker could use this vulnerability to perform different attacks. These could include redirecting the user to a malicious web site where he may be tricked into inputting private information or a key logger using malicious code to steal authentication and other privileged material.

Unauthorized Access by Parameter Manipulation

Risk level: **HIGH**

This vulnerability involves having a potential security weakness to what is called a parameter manipulation attack. The problem is inherent in input fields, where too many choices of search parameters are given to users without sufficient controls over the parameters they may choose. This may allow a user unintended privileges in accessing parameters, such as session tokens, values stored in cookies, HTTP headers, and so on. A malicious user could exploit this vulnerability to access and gather data about other valid users. This could result in breaches to confidentiality and privacy.

A parameter manipulation attack compromises weak protection of data residing in a user's browser, where that data should otherwise be invisible and unable to be changed by a user. The data can be session tokens, values stored in cookies, HTTP headers, or even prices in web carts.

Buffer Overflows

Risk level: **HIGH**

Buffer overflows are a high-risk vulnerability that are widely publicized and should be avoided.

Web applications may be vulnerable to buffer overflows, which occur when a program attempts to store more data in a static buffer than it is designed to manage. The additional data overwrites and corrupts memory, allowing an attacker to insert arbitrary instructions on the web server or crash the system. For additional clarity, a buffer overflow is an error that may occur when a program writes more data than expected to a buffer or space allocated for an expected amount of data. The excess data overruns the buffer's boundary and overwrites adjacent memory. If this violation is allowed to occur, it can permit a hacker to inject instructions and compromise an environment.

Applications may be susceptible to the insertion of too much data, which may cause a memory overflow. This may allow dangerous instructions to be input. For example, a hacker may enter a command line executable statement such as

```
<! -exec%20cmd="/bin/cat%20/etc/passwd"->
```

into a legitimate web site form under the guise of an HTTP request to gain access to the web server. If security configuration allows, the hacker will receive the /etc/passwd file and gain access to files and, ultimately, the usernames and passwords stored on the web server.

Forms Submitted Using the GET Method

Risk level: **HIGH**

This vulnerability is almost identical to the previously discussed vulnerability of submitting data using the GET method. In this case, an entire form is submitted using the GET method.

This is a common security vulnerability we see, where a number of the web forms are submitted using the GET method. The GET method is considered insecure because it visibly presents the submitted parameters and their values in the browser address bar. A malicious user can exploit this vulnerability and perform a man-in-the-middle attack, where she uses the visible information to impersonate either the browser to the web application or the web application to the browser. An attacker could also do a parameter manipulation attack by manipulating parameters within the visible URL text to gain access to unauthorized data.

Redirects and Forwards to Insecure Sites

Risk level: **LOW-MEDIUM**

A session being redirected to an insecure web site is even more serious than users surfing to the same dangerous page on their own, simply because there is an implied trust relationship between the user and the page doing the redirecting.

Web applications frequently redirect and forward users to other pages and web sites and use untrusted data to determine the destination pages. Without proper validation, attackers can redirect victims to phishing or malware sites or use forwards to access unauthorized pages.

Maliciously installed redirects may attempt to install malware or trick victims into disclosing passwords or other sensitive information and may facilitate the bypass of access control by an attacker.

Application Susceptible to Brute-Force Attacks

Risk level: **LOW**

This vulnerability arises when the application code does not stop a potentially malicious user from gaining unauthorized access after a certain number of failed authentication attempts, simply by denying access for a period of time or forever.

If the attacker's false login attempts are not restricted after several attempts, the attacker can proceed to discover a successful username and password combination and use it to impersonate the account's legitimate user, thereby gaining unauthorized access to the application.

Client-Side Enforcement of Server-Side Security

Risk level: **MEDIUM**

When validation is performed on the client side, security is always affected to some extent because it allows for much less control than when it is enforced on the server side.

If a server relies on validation mechanisms placed on the client side, an attacker can modify the client-side behavior to bypass the protection mechanisms, resulting in potentially unexpected interactions between the client and server. The consequences will vary depending on what the mechanisms are trying to protect.

Injection Flaws

Risk level: **HIGH**

Injection vulnerability is caused by a lack of sufficient filtering or testing of data; that is, input from a client. All data other than expected items such as size, type, and character type should be rejected by the web application immediately.

This is a class of attacks that relies on injecting data into a web application in order to facilitate the execution or interpretation of malicious data in an unexpected manner. Examples of attacks within this class include cross-site scripting (XSS), SQL injection, header injection, and many more. They result in running malicious code to steal and compromise data.

Malicious instructions are included with user data and sent as part of a command or query to an interpreter, which is a program used to convert high-level language commands into machine-readable binary language, in a line-by-line fashion, in near real time as part of a command or query. The attacker's hostile instructions can trick the interpreter into executing unintended commands or accessing data without proper authorization.

In these attacks, the victims are web applications and the databases behind them, but can also include the users of a vulnerable web site.

Five different injection vulnerabilities follow.

SQL Injection

Risk level: **HIGH**

A SQL injection is one of several types of injection vulnerabilities, which allows malicious SQL statements and queries to be submitted to a web application without the web application stripping them out.

Many web applications do not properly strip user input of unnecessary special characters, such as string literal escape characters, nor do they validate information contained in a web request before making SQL queries. SQL injection is an attack technique that takes advantage of a security vulnerability in a web application to extract or alter data within the database management system, which resides at the back end of the web application. The data may come from an input field on a client's web browser as part of a command or request. The data is then used for doing SQL queries or executing commands in a back-end database that are never intended to occur in normal activity. If the vulnerability to this attack allows the database to respond to the malicious instructions, the database is compromised. A less direct attack injects malicious code into strings that will be kept in a table for future reference. When the stored strings are subsequently used in an SQL command, the malicious code is executed.

Such attacks can result in access to unauthorized data, bypassing of authentication, or the shutting down of a database regardless of whether the database resides on the web server or a separate server.

Blind SQL Injection

Risk level: **HIGH**

A blind SQL injection is another flavor of an injection vulnerability, where a web application does not filter or restrict requests for more information from the back-end database. These types of requests should be very closely filtered by developers.

Blind SQL injection differs from a normal SQL injection in the way the data is retrieved from the database. When the database does not output data to the web page and instead displays an error message about the syntax of the query, an attacker is forced to steal data by asking the database a series of true or false questions. This makes exploiting the SQL injection vulnerability more difficult, but still possible.

The risks are the same as for other SQL injection attacks.

Link Injection

Risk level: **HIGH**

This attack occurs when a malicious user is allowed to input code that contains carriage return (CR) and line feed (LF) characters into an HTTP RESPONSE header. After the characters are injected, the attacker makes space in the header to write their own malicious code. The malicious data in the HTTP header is then passed to the web application via the client's browser.

This vulnerability facilitates a cross-site request forgery attack, which is covered later in this chapter.

HTTP Header Injection Vulnerability

Risk level: **HIGH**

An HTTP header injection vulnerability occurs when HTTP headers are created on the fly based upon user input. This vulnerability occurs if strict filtering is not put in place to restrict malicious characters. The vulnerability can allow for the HTTP response-splitting attack to occur. An HTTP response header includes detailed information about an HTTP sent or received message, which a typical user never sees but is quite available to view on a browser. Viewing the header information is accomplished either by using the appropriate command or getting the appropriate viewing tool for any web browser.

HTTP Response-Splitting Attack

Risk level: **HIGH**

The HTTP response-splitting attack compromises the HTTP header and is another member of the injection vulnerability class. It occurs when insufficient filtering allows the carriage return (CR) character and line feed (LF) character to be entered into the

HTTP header if the underlying environment is vulnerable to these characters. If attackers can inject CR or LF line characters into the header, then they can also inject new HTTP headers and write arbitrary content into the application's response.

An attacker can exploit this vulnerability to mount an attack using multiple attack vectors. This type of attack can lead to a full systems compromise and loss of confidentiality, integrity, and availability.

Any attack that can be delivered via cross-site scripting can usually also be delivered via header injection because the attacker can construct a request that causes arbitrary JavaScript to appear within the response body. Further, it is sometimes possible to leverage header injection vulnerabilities to poison the cache of any proxy server through which users access the application. Here, an attacker sends a crafted request that results in a "split" response containing arbitrary content. JavaScript is a scripting language developed by Netscape to enable web authors to design interactive sites. It shares many of the features and structures of the full Java language but it also can interact with HTML source code, enabling dynamic content to be created.

If the proxy server can be manipulated to associate the injected response with another URL used within the application, then the attacker can perform a "stored" attack against this URL that will compromise other users who request that URL in the future.

Unauthorized View of Data

Risk level: **LOW-HIGH**

This is a common vulnerability, where sensitive information about the web application environment is disclosed. This can assist a hacker in probing for more sensitive data in preparation for an attack. The vulnerability arises when an unauthorized user identifies an object such as a server or file name by a specific name. An indirect reference is done by providing an alias name to the server or file, such as a number value or a description of what the device does. This way, users only see alias names and the application environment translates between alias names and real object names. If authorization for each user is not verified prior to accessing an object, a malicious party could gain confidential information about the environment, sufficient to plan an attack.

In actual audit situations, we have seen this particular problem, with web application pages using the formal names of objects. Without an access control check or other protection, attackers can manipulate these references and guess names of other objects in order to access unauthorized data. This vulnerability can be compromised by both an authorized and unauthorized user.

Web Application Source Code Disclosure

Risk level: **LOW**

This is a similar vulnerability to unauthorized view of data, but in this case it is specifically related to actually revealing pieces of source code. Source code is the set of instructions written in a programming language that regulate what an application does and how it should operate. Application source code should not be accessible to web users, as it may contain sensitive application information and back-end logic. This is not an unusual occurrence, as we detected responses containing fragments of application source code during separate audits.

While such leakage does not necessarily represent a breach in security, it can give an attacker useful guidance for future exploitation. Leakage of sensitive data may carry various levels of risk and should be limited whenever possible.

Web Directories Enumerated

Risk level: **LOW**

This unauthorized view is specifically related to web directories and involves confidential information pertaining to names of directories and their subdirectories being made available to users. This information, in the hands of a malicious person, can be used to plan an attack.

It is often the case when we do vulnerability scans of external IP addresses that we are able to enumerate several web directories. An attacker would most likely focus on these directories (especially the ones with names that reveal the function of objects within each directory) and try to fine-tune an attack accordingly.

Active Directory Object Default Page on Server

Risk level: **LOW**

An Active Directory object default page contains information that should only be seen by the developers of a web application environment, but definitely not by web application users. This information can be inadvertently revealed to users as the result of incorrect parameter settings by developers.

Active Directory is a very widely used Microsoft Windows service that provides a way to view and organize all the network resources, particularly for a complex and large environment, in a digestible manner. Active Directory objects are all the bits and pieces that the service organizes, such as users, computers, groups of users, supersets of groups of users called organizational units (OU), and so on.

A malicious party could build on information details about network devices and the application to fine-tune an attack. This reduces an attacker's workload by reducing the attack scope and risk of detection while increasing the probability of a successful attack.

Temporary Files Left in the Environment

Risk level: **LOW**

Here is another example of sensitive information being inadvertently made available to a potential hacker and becoming a security vulnerability. In this case, the knowledge relates to temporary files. Web application users can gain access to pages containing temporary files simply by exploring web links. Although the temporary files are required by the application, they should be accessible only to authorized users. Temporary files are files typically used during an update or editing process. Once the process is complete, the user saves the changes and the files get closed or deleted. However, if there are of unplanned activities, such as restarting a computer or turning it off during an active Windows session, the files may get left in the environment.

If the temporary files are found by a malicious party, confidential data may be revealed. Further, if any of the temporary files can be written to by an attacker, malicious code can be injected into it, and it may be vulnerable to being moved to a location that inherently gives the attacker more access privileges. Finally, the script files for a temporary file may reveal the application logic and other sensitive information such as usernames and passwords.

Internal IP Address Revealed by Web Server

Risk level: **MEDIUM**

This is the old story of too much information being revealed to an unintended, unauthorized individual. In this case, an IP address is the item of concern and could be used by a hacker to build an attack.

For example, if a web server is misconfigured and identifies its internal IP address in an HTTP header field, that IP address could allow unauthorized parties to learn potentially dangerous information about the corporate network.

If an attacker knows the address space of the internal network, she may be able to craft packets to get around network protection (firewall, intrusion detection systems/intrusion prevention systems) and get access to the insecure internal network.

Server Path Disclosed

Risk level: **MEDIUM**

Another instance of otherwise-confidential information being revealed to any unauthorized individual, in this case a literal file path is disclosed and could be used by a hacker to build an attack.

For example, an HTTP response containing a file's absolute path (e.g., c:\dir\file in Windows or /dir/file in UNIX) may be clearly visible. An unauthorized party may be able to exploit this information to access sensitive data on the directory structure of the server machine, which it could then use for further attacks against the site.

Information such as the location of files on the server as well as directory structure may be extremely beneficial for an attacker. It could allow the attacker to craft and fine-tune an attack that will have a higher probability of success while reducing the effort and elapsed time required to execute it.

Hidden Directory Detected

Risk level: **LOW**

Hidden directories are another type of directory information, which are intended for viewing only by developers and have no business in the hands of web application users. They are a directory (folder), such as an Active Directory or other types of directories, that file system utilities do not display by default. They are commonly used for storing user preferences and the states of various tools or utilities.

The web application exposes the presence of the hidden directory on the web application server by issuing a 403 Forbidden Response code in response to users attempting to access this directory without having access authorization.

Although the directory does not list its content, any available pieces of data could reveal sufficient information for an attacker to develop an attack against the site. For example, by knowing the directory name, an attacker could guess the content type and possibly file names that reside in it, or subdirectories under it, and try to access them.

Unencrypted VIEWSTATE

Risk level: **HIGH**

Here is another instance of revealing too much information, in this case unencrypted confidential data sent by a browser to its server. As a reminder, VIEWSTATE is a temporary storage that allows ASP.NET users to store all the temporary information about a web page, such as which panels are open and in use, the options that are currently chosen, the current data in each text box, and even the data for other information.

During an audit, we were able to see confidential material from the browser session being sent back to the application in an unencrypted view state. Therefore, any user can see information for which he does not have sufficient authorization.

Obsolete Web Server

Risk level: **MEDIUM**

Obsolete servers can be more vulnerable to attacks since they do not have the most up-to-date security protection. An attacker could exploit this vulnerability to mount an attack focused on known vulnerabilities in outdated versions of the web site platform. Such an attack has a higher likelihood of success on this version than on a more secure version.

There are just too many real-life examples of this occurring, not only for web servers but for all manner of servers.

Query Parameter in SSL Request

Risk level: **MEDIUM**

This is another variation of a vulnerability that can occur when developers use the GET command instead of using other commands such as POST, which presents fewer security risks. The GET method allows for requests to be stored in a browser's history.

A vulnerability arises when the browser's history is used to reveal the URLs containing the query parameter names and values. If these names and values are not confidential, then the confidential information is available to unauthorized parties.

During several web application vulnerability tests, we found HTTP GET requests in browser histories that contained parameters containing confidential information.

Error Handling

Risk level: **HIGH**

This is a variation on the theme of revealing what may appear to be innocuous information to unauthorized parties. In reality, a competent hacker may be able to leverage the information while preparing an attack.

A malicious party may intentionally submit abnormal data in order to force error messages. An attacker could use generic error messages such as "Username incorrect" and "Password incorrect" or hidden files and directories to plan an attack.

Cross-Site Scripting Attacks

Risk level: **HIGH**

Cross-site scripting (XSS) attacks receive a lot of news coverage, principally because of the dramatic increase in the use of scripting languages. The same-old problems creep up even in these relatively new scripting languages—insufficient filtering of input data from users and, conversely, banning all but expected types of data.

This XSS vulnerability is caused by flaws in client-side scripting languages such as JavaScript and the HTML scripting language. It can arise when web applications accept input data from users and dynamically include it in web pages without properly validating it first. XSS vulnerabilities allow an attacker to execute arbitrary commands and display arbitrary content in a user's browser. In the victim's browser, the malicious code appears to be a legitimate part of a web site and causes it to act as an unintentional accomplice to the attacker.

Cross-site scripting is the most prevalent web application security flaw. XSS flaws occur when an application includes user-supplied data in a page sent to the browser without properly validating or rejecting it. There are three known types of XSS flaws:

- stored
- reflected
- DOM based

The consequences of an XSS attack are the same regardless of the type of flaw, with the difference between them only in how the payload arrives at the server.

The damaging results of the XSS attack include: user sessions being hijacked to steal or to change confidential information, defacement of web sites, insertion of hostile content, redirection of users, disclosure of the end user's session token, and the platform on which the user's browser is running being attacked.

Reflected Cross-Site Scripting Attack

Risk level: **HIGH**

In a reflected XSS attack, malicious data enters a client's browser by the browser making a request to a compromised web site. The browser becomes infected with malicious malware code. When the client then accesses its trusted web application, the malware on the browser secretly requests personal information from the web site. The web site sends or reflects the data to the compromised browser, which in turn sends the personal information to the attacker.

The most common mechanism for delivering malicious content is to include it as a parameter in a URL that is posted publicly or e-mailed directly to the victim. URLs constructed in this manner constitute the core of many phishing schemes, involving an attacker convincing a victim to visit a URL that refers her to a vulnerable site. Once the victim is on the site, the attacker will cause malicious code to execute within the user's browser.

The attacker-supplied code can perform a wide variety of actions, such as stealing the victim's session token or login credentials, performing arbitrary actions on the victim's behalf, and logging her keystrokes. The attacker can induce a user to issue his crafted request by:

- Requesting the transfer of private information, such as cookies that include session data, from the victim's computer to that of the attacker, who then can hijack the session

- Sending malicious requests to a web site, which could be especially dangerous if the victim has administrator privileges

- Conducting phishing attacks that emulate trusted web sites and trick the victim into entering a password, allowing the attacker to compromise the victim's account

- Exploiting browser vulnerabilities that enable the attacker to take over the victim's computer (drive-by hacking)

Stored Cross-Site Scripting Attack

Risk level: **HIGH**

In this attack, the malicious code is stored permanently on the compromised web application, such as in the back-end database. In a compromise situation, when a client's browser retrieves information from the compromised web site, it also retrieves malware. In this case, there are two sets of victims: the compromised web site and the visitors to the compromised web site. The order of the attack sequence is:

1. The attacker inserts malicious code into a web application.

2. The victim, who is a client of the web site, requests a page from the web site.

3. The compromised web site unwittingly sends the malicious code to its client's browser.

4. The compromised client's browser sends confidential information back to the attacker's server.

Cross-Site Request Forgery Attack

Risk level: **HIGH**

Cross-site request forgery (CSRF) is yet another vulnerability caused by insufficient filtering of data input into a web application. This complex attack dupes a browser into being an unwitting participant in an attack against an otherwise-trusted web site. This type of attack sounds like the XSS attack just defined. However, it differs from XSS in that here the attacker uses the victim's browser as a conduit through which to send malicious instructions to a web application currently authenticating the victim. In this case, there are two concurrent victims:

- the client whose browser is being remotely controlled by the attacker, who is an unwitting participant in the attack

- the trusted web site to which the client browser is authenticated, which is the ultimate victim of the attack

The CSRF attack forces a logged-on victim's browser to send a forged HTTP request, which includes the victim's session cookie and any other automatically included authentication information, to a vulnerable web application. The attacker forces the victim's browser to generate seemingly legitimate requests and send them to the vulnerable application. In the security world, a cookie is used as a messenger to carry session identification data related to a specific session. The session identification is called a session cookie or session token or session identifier.

CSRF takes advantage of the fact that most web apps allow potential attackers to predict all the details of a particular action. Since browsers send credentials like session cookies automatically, attackers can create malicious web pages that generate forged requests indistinguishable from the legitimate ones.

Security Misconfigurations and Use of Known Vulnerable Components

Risk level: **MEDIUM**

It is imperative for operations teams dealing with web applications to ensure their configurations of hardware and software are free of known vulnerabilities. However, we have commonly seen misconfigurations that expose web applications to threats. This issue is exacerbated because there is a huge volume of documented security vulnerabilities, primarily published in good faith for the benefit of protecting applications and networks but also serving as guidance for hackers. Off-the-shelf and widely available software components such as libraries, frameworks, and other software modules can have security weaknesses that are able to be exploited by parties with malicious intent. The problem is exacerbated if these components run with full privileges. If a vulnerable component is exploited, such an attack can facilitate serious data loss or server takeover. This is a common problem, as few development teams focus on ensuring that their components/libraries are up to date.

The full range of weaknesses is therefore possible, including injection, broken access control, cross-site scripting, and so forth. The impact could range from minimal to complete host takeover and data compromise.

Denial-of-Service Attack

Risk level: **HIGH**

Many web applications are vulnerable to denial-of-service (DoS) attacks that can dramatically curtail access or even result in a total shutdown of the affected network. Attackers can use various mechanisms to launch a DOS attack, such as sending many TCP requests and using an Internet control message protocol (ICMP) to flood a device with ping requests. ICMP is a fundamental Internet protocol; in this case, it is used by devices on a network to send error and control messages back and forth to each other. ICMP flooding is malicious use of the ICMP protocol to deluge a target device with so many messages as to overwhelm its ability to respond or to therefore properly function.

Excessive numbers of TCP and ICMP ping requests, which are simply various flavors of Internet traffic, are very high generators of unnecessary traffic. When used as designed, these protocols work well; misused, they are tools for DoS attacks. DoS attacks may be simple, such as repeated requests for a single URL from a single source, or more complex, such as a coordinated effort from multiple machines or botnets to barrage the URL.

Related Security Issues

Risk level: **HIGH**

There are several security issues that can be sources of the previous vulnerabilities of which users should be aware.

Storage of Data at Rest

Risk level: **HIGH**

People are very concerned about data in motion, such as data and web sites, being compromised during transactions. However, there is also an entire class of vulnerabilities associated with data at rest, such as the security used to store data associated with web applications.

Many web application logs contain sensitive information, such as passwords, session IDs, web server requests, and statistics, and by default many applications provide logs that detail the product's installation data. These logs and other sensitive files may be stored on the web server or back-end database and hackers can retrieve them to perform unauthorized functions, view their content, or compromise the resource.

Storage of Account Lists

Risk level: **HIGH**

Hackers can also use account information to plan an attack. Identifying usernames by their accounts is a strong tool to leverage if this opportunity presents itself.

Here are several real-life examples of vulnerabilities associated with account information we obtained during the course of one audit:

- an account list stored in a file with minimum security controls

- an account list containing many stale accounts, including previous employees and contractors no longer providing services for the company

- the event log for an account file indicating several failed attempts by existing employees at logging into stale accounts

Password Storage

Risk level: **HIGH**

Gaining valid credentials for an application is bread and butter for a hacker. The ability to gain even hints about how passwords are built and stored is valuable for a hacker who is building an attack.

Most applications have a password recovery system that is activated by clicking on the password reminder link. This identifies the fact that passwords are stored or encrypted as plain text. This unsecure form of storage may allow an attacker to gain access to passwords, which, in combination with a valid username, could provide unauthorized access to confidential corporate information including a client's personal and sensitive data.

Since this type of application is also susceptible to SQL injection, the password list is definitely at risk. A successful SQL injection attack would make the plain text or encrypted passwords vulnerable to exposure.

Insufficient Patch Management

Risk level: **HIGH**

One of the most common and high-risk activities an operations team can commit is to not install security-related patches in a timely manner. Since descriptions of vulnerabilities and their associated patches or corrections are widely published to assist with security, the same information is just as available to potential hackers.

During the network-vulnerability portion of our audit, we identified out-of-date revision levels in several third-party software platforms associated with the web application environment.

This may be indicative of an insufficient patch-management process. Since insufficient/insecure patches result in a very large percentage of web application vulnerabilities, this section needs to be included as part of a web application vulnerability list.

Summary

There are many well-known and clearly documented classes of web application vulnerabilities. Each class of vulnerability contains well-documented members of its class.

There will undoubtedly be more classes and class members that evolve right along with changes in web application infrastructure and the progression of creative cyberattacks. The cyberattackers will in turn create threats to compromise these vulnerabilities, thereby creating new risk.

The documented remediations for all these classes and class members are the subject of Chapter 4.

CHAPTER 4

■ ■ ■

Web Application Vulnerabilities and Countermeasures

Chapter 3 identified many commonly found vulnerabilities in my real experience as an auditor. This chapter explains how to remediate each vulnerability. For both chapters, the vulnerabilities and their remediations are grouped into classes or variations on a theme of susceptibility. The classes are:

- authentication
- session management
- access control
- input validation
- redirects and forwards
- injection flaws
- unauthorized view of data
- error handling
- cross-site scripting
- security misconfigurations
- denial of service
- related security issues

For brevity and clarity, in this chapter the recommendations for eliminating each vulnerability are provided in list form following a brief introduction.

■ **Note** A summary table featuring the vulnerability class definitions from Chapter 3 and the remediations discussed in this chapter is available in spreadsheet format with the downloads for this book. See the Source Code/Downloads tab on the book's Apress product page: www.apress.com/9781484201497.

Lack of Sufficient Authentication

Risk level: **HIGH**

The hacker's mantra is acquiring unauthorized access. The mantra of the security manager is to provide strong authentication and to force all potential users to provide strong evidence as to who they are and to what degree of access they are entitled. This section deals mainly with the front-end process of identification and how to not unnecessarily reveal secrets that could compromise authentication. The back end of this process is associating users with what privileges they are entitled to, but the details of implementing and enforcing credentials is beyond the scope of this chapter.

It is important to ensure there is a corporate authentication policy. The policy should specify all aspects of authentication, including password management, designation of privileges, and the prevention of leakage of confidential information relating to authentication. The policy should also specify the requirements that will be used to guarantee the adherence of the security department, IT operations, and all users. Some of these requirements include:

- **Password strength**: Passwords should have restrictions that require a minimum size and complexity. Complexity typically involves the combinations of alphabetic, numeric, and/or nonalphanumeric characters (e.g., at least one of each) in a password. (See the "Weak Password Controls" section.)

- **Password use**: Users should be restricted to a certain number of login attempts per unit of time. Repeated failed login attempts should be logged. Passwords provided during failed login attempts should not be recorded, as this may expose a user's password to whoever can gain access to this log.

- **Nondescriptive error messages**: The system should not indicate whether it was the username or password that was wrong if a login attempt fails.

- **Failed login attempt notification**: Users should be informed of the date/time of their last successful login and the number of failed attempts to access their account since that time.

- **Password change controls**: Users should be required to change their password periodically and should be prevented from reusing previous passwords. There should be requirements for doing so, including:

  - A password change mechanism should be used wherever users are allowed to change a password, regardless of the situation.

  - Users should always be required to provide both their old and new password when changing their password (like all account information).

  - The system should require users to reauthenticate whenever changing their e-mail address—otherwise any attacker who might temporarily get access to their session (e.g., by walking up to their computer while they are logged in) can simply change their e-mail address and request a "forgotten" password be mailed to them.

- **Strong authentication, including authentication tokens**: Strong authentication, such as HTTPS, with encrypted credentials should be employed. While authentication to a web application typically involves the use of a user ID and password, stronger methods of authentication are also commercially available such as software- and hardware-based cryptographic tokens or biometrics.

- **Required reauthentication**: Reauthentication should be required at specified time intervals or when users move between web pages.

- **Testing and enforcement of authentication**: Authentication and all potential ways to circumvent it should be regularly tested. A user privilege policy should be enforced, specifying what authenticated users are and are not allowed to do.

Weak Password Controls

Risk level: **HIGH**

Because passwords are one of the most important elements to Internet security, they must be protected and changed regularly. The first requirement is that the password cannot be identical to the previous 13 passwords. A policy for enforcing password complexity also should be implemented, with the minimum requirements of

- at least one nonalphanumeric character

- at least two numeric characters

- at least two uppercase letters

- at least two lowercase letters

Passwords Submitted Without Encryption

Risk level: **HIGH**

Since passwords are susceptible to theft, it should be ensured that they are protected by encryption or by hashing, which is a form of one-way encryption.

All passwords should be hashed for session authentication as well as during transmission. Additionally, passwords should be stored as hashed values when the data is at rest.

Username Harvesting

Risk level: **HIGH**

Since in two-factor authentication, the other critical component besides a password is the username, usernames should always be kept confidential and should not be inadvertently made available for potential hackers to harvest (steal). To mitigate harvesting, confidential information about usernames and passwords should not be inadvertently disclosed, as might happen in:

- **Error messages**: Error messages should be user friendly, but they are also required to be ambiguous and uninformative, especially for unauthenticated users.

- **Login-screen error messages**: Any error message in the login screen should be along the lines of "User name or password is incorrect."

- **Forgot Password screen**: The error message in the Forgot Password screen should specifically avoid identifying which that a registered user's information is stored in the system database.

Weak Session Management

Risk level: **LOW-HIGH**

All transactions or sessions between a client web browser and a web application must be encrypted as a basic security measure. This will reduce the chance of sensitive data and the session being compromised. To do this:

- *Encrypt all transactions.* All transactions between web browsers and web applications must be encrypted with the Security Sockets Layer (SSL) or TLS protocol so that your application will run on an SSL/HTTPS-secured site.

- *Ensure the SSL or TLS version you are using is up to date.* After testing them, only the most current security patches should be implemented to make sure they do not cause any problems. Using an outdated version of the SSL/TLS with known security vulnerabilities is a security red flag.

- *Obtain SSL or TLS certificates from a trusted certificate authority.* The root certificates with their public key should be installed in any web application platform or operating system.

- *Do not use homemade or self-signed certificates.* Industry-trusted certificates are simply more secure than self-signed certificates.

- *Encrypt or hash as appropriate all security-related data at rest, such as keys, certificates, and passwords.* Unencrypted high-risk data, particularly data in motion, is simply too important to not secure with encryption or with hashing.

- *Ensure secure storage of secrets in memory.* Developers must adhere to processes for scrubbing confidential data that exists in memory at the end of sessions. It is important to ensure that any long-term data storage is adequately protected by implementing strong authentication on a need-to-access basis.

- *Approve algorithms for SSL or TLS.* Do not use any algorithms other than industry-approved ones. Keep your algorithm choice updated. No homegrown algorithms, ever.

- *Choose approved algorithms and randomize them.* Choose randomizing algorithms for use by SSL or TLS that are approved by security experts and are subject to public scrutiny.

- *Choose approved ciphers.* Similarly, choose expert-approved and publicly scrutinized ciphers for use by SSL OR TLS.

- *Ensure that initiation is only from within HTTPS.* Ensure that web site access or data transfer can only initiated from within an HTTPS connection.

- *Test for restricted access control within a web site.* Test the web site to see whether access can be initiated or data transfer can occur anywhere on the site that has an HTTP connection, and if it can, migrate to HTTPS.

Weak SSL Ciphers Support

Risk level: **HIGH**

Secure Socket Layer (SSL) is a security measure that needs to be configured with its most secure, up-to-date options; in this case, by choosing a strong cipher option. Reconfigure the web server to use only a strong cipher suite for SSL.

Information Submitted Using the GET Method

Risk level: **MEDIUM**

Several ways exist to make and submit requests within HTTP; some are less secure than others. Two methods for a request-response between a client and server within HTTP are GET and POST. In order to optimize the security of HTTP communications, all forms submitting passwords should use the POST method for submitting data to be processed to a specific resource. To achieve this, use POST (method="POST") for the FORM tag. It may also be necessary to modify the corresponding server-side form handler to ensure that submitted passwords are properly retrieved from the message body rather than from a URL query string.

In a nutshell:

- **GET**: Requests data from a specified resource. It is less secure, as it writes requests in the URL in the form of a URL query string.

- **POST**: Submits data to be processed to a specified resource. POST is more secure than a GET command, as it stores request data in the body of a message and not in a URL string. Also, the POST query strings are not stored in browser history or in web server logs.

Self-Signed Certificates, Insecure Keys, and Passwords

Risk level: **HIGH**

Any stored confidential information is subject to compromise. The best policy is to minimize the amount of stored critical information and only keep information that is absolutely necessary. A few tips for storage follow:

- *Instead of storing information, require users to re-enter it.* Rather than encrypting and storing credit card numbers or other critical information with a high threat value, simply require users to re-enter the information during each new session.

- *Hash, don't encrypt, passwords.* Hashing is used to verify the accuracy and validity of data. Instead of storing encrypted passwords, use a one-way function such as SHA-1 to hash the passwords. Hashed values are much more difficult to convert to readable plain text than encrypted values. Hashing is a one-direction-only method of encrypting short amounts of data by using a hashing algorithm that cannot be decrypted. The way it works is that two parties use the same hashing algorithm on the same confidential data, such as a password, in order to create hashed values. The two hashed values are then compared, and if they are the same, then both parties have agreed to the validity of the confidential information. In this way, no confidential information is actually ever shared or transmitted.

- *Encrypt all critical information.* Encryption is used to hide information that is meant to be accessed only by intended recipients, and so it has a very different use than hashing. Choose an encryption algorithm that has been exposed to public scrutiny and make sure that there are no open vulnerabilities. Encapsulate the cryptographic functions that are used and review the code carefully. Be sure that secrets, such as keys, certificates, passwords, and application logs, are stored securely.

- *Divide the master secret for encryption keys between at least two locations and assemble them at runtime.* Such locations might include a configuration file, an external server, or a place within the code itself.

Username Harvesting Applied to Forgotten Password Process

Risk level: **HIGH**

Although error messages should be user friendly, they should also be ambiguous and uninformative, especially for unauthenticated users. The authentication error message should be the same for all users and should be along the lines of "User password could not be reset."

Autocomplete Enabled on Password Fields

Risk level: **LOW**

To prevent browsers from storing credentials entered into HTML forms, the attribute should be configured as autocomplete="off" within the FORM tag (to protect all form fields) or within the relevant INPUT tags (to protect specific individual fields).

Session IDs Nonrandom and Too Short

Risk level: **MEDIUM**

You should use a random session ID with a length of at least 128 bits (16 bytes). More information is available at www.owasp.org/index.php/Session_Management_Cheat_Sheet#Session_ID_Properties.

Weak Access Control

Risk level: **LOW-HIGH**

Restricting access to only authorized users is core to strong application security. We will look at the requirements for limiting access to a web application and its server here.

For every application function:

- *Do not allow unauthorized access to an application.* Ensure that unauthorized users cannot gain access to functions to which they should not have access at the application level.

- *Restrict unauthorized access to a server.* Ensure unauthorized users cannot gain access to functions to which they should not have access at the server level.

- *Verify authentication with server-side information.* Ensure that server-side checks on authentication can be independently verified without information initiated solely on the client side, such as by verifying the user IP address with credentials.

- *Test authentication of roles with various privileges.* Use a proxy with maximum privileges to browse the applications. Then revisit restricted pages using a less privileged role. The server responses should be more restrictive for the less privileged role. If this is not the case, insufficient authentication enforcement may be indicated.

- *Utilize a single, unified authentication scheme.* Use a single, unified authentication mechanism and single storage facility for all authentication and privileges by function throughout the entire web application infrastructure.

- *Ensure simplicity of management of privileges.* Make sure that the authentication mechanism provides for easy management of privileges by function according to user or user group.

- *Deny access by default.* Ensure that enforcement mechanisms deny all access by default by requiring that access to every function is explicitly granted for specific roles.

- *Test all logic functions.* Prior to allowing access, test all logical/if conditions to ensure that for all functions involved in the workflow all conditions are in the proper state.

- *Do not reveal unauthorized information.* Do not show links or buttons to users who do not have authority to use these functions.

Frameable Response (Clickjacking)

Risk level: **LOW**

Frames are a convenient tool for developers to divide a screen into sections, but they must be well secured or they pose security risks. To do so:

- *Carefully secure framing.* Require the application to either return a response header with the name of any frame used, return IFrame or X-Frame options with the value DENY to prevent framing altogether, or return the value SAMEORIGIN to allow framing only by pages with the same origin as the response itself. For clarity, frames, IFrames, and X-Frames are additional tools available to web site developers that allow a developer to divide a screen into different sections so that each section can get information from its own separate information source.

- *Use the latest web server version.* It is recommended to upgrade to the latest web server version available and to verify that the version effectively deals with the framing issue.

Cached HTTP Response

Risk level: **MEDIUM**

Cache is used to speed up response time. As typically used in the context of this book, it refers to clumps of often-accessed data stored within a user's browser or in memory for the sole purpose of reducing the need for a browser or a program to execute a slower query into the main memory of a server. Caching means faster speeds, but it also has the inherent security risk of being compromised while holding confidential information.

Due to the confidentiality issues involved, a web application should return caching directives instructing browsers not to store local copies of any sensitive data. Often, this can be achieved by configuring the web server to prevent caching for relevant paths within the web root. Alternatively, most web development platforms allow control of the server's caching directives from within individual scripts. Ideally, the web server should return the following HTTP headers in all responses containing sensitive content:

```
Cache-control: no-storePragma: no-cache
```

HTTP messages have a structure that includes options that a developer can choose between. The options are similar to menu selections in a restaurant. One of the options is called Cache-Control. A developer may choose to allow or not allow caching with the Cache-Control header option. Pragma is the legacy HTTP/1.0 implementation for managing cache, and Cache-Control is the HTTP/1.1 implementation for cache control. They both prevent the client browser from caching a response. Older clients may not support HTTP/1.1, which is why that header is still in use. Caching, or storing, information within a client browser is used to improve response speed. In cases where privileged information such as passwords is cached, security vulnerabilities are created.

In situations where legacy HTTP 1.0 servers do not support the Cache-Control headers, the HTTP Pragma: No-Cache header can be used. However, Pragma: No-Cache can prevent caching only if it is used for an SSL page.

The best way to implement Pragma: No-Cache is to place another header just before the HTML code ends. This way, the browser will parse the Pragma: No-Cache directive after the complete page has been loaded. The reason for this is the Pragma: No-Cache directive is used in the Meta tag in the header, which is normally at the beginning of an HTML web page.

When an HTML code is parsed (in a top-to-bottom approach), the browser looks for the presence of the page in the cache as soon as it reads the Pragma directive. But since at that moment the page has not been cached (a web page gets cached only after it has filled at least 32 kilobytes of the buffer), the browser will not clear the cache and it will go ahead with parsing the rest of the code. As a result, all the contents of web page that are loaded after the parsing of Pragma get cached.

Sensitive Information Disclosed in HTML Comments

Risk level: **LOW**

Similarly to not allowing information about HTTP sessions to remain on a computer, there should be no sensitive information stored on the web site or web application, as it could be viewed by a potential hacker. To ensure that this does not happen, check all HTML comments for:

- vital information, including file names and file paths

- previous (or future) site links

- sensitive information

- source code fragments

HTTP Server Type and Version Number Disclosed

Risk level: **LOW**

Similar to the caution of disclosing unnecessary information about a web application environment, you want to avoid revealing information specific to the make and model of the web server. Modify the web server response to include only the minimum information required by the client-side application. Several tools and utilities can be used to perform this operation.

Insufficient Session Expiration

Risk level: **MEDIUM**

Sessions need to be set to expire after the completion of a session, during periods of inactivity, and after a predetermined maximum amount of time in order to minimize the potential of a hacker gaining access to session information or hijacking a session. Session expiration should include:

- **Inactivity expiration**: Ensure that each session expires automatically after a sufficient amount of time of inactivity.

- **Absolute time-out**: Ensure that each session expires automatically after a defined amount of time.

- **Deletion of session information**: Ensure that session information is destroyed on the client and server side upon user logout.

- **Validation of new users**: Enforce the invalidation of all existing session identifiers prior to authorizing a new user session.

HTML Does Not Specify Charset

Risk level: **LOW**

It is important for web application developers to specify which character set, or charset, they want used within HTML content, as some sets are more prone to security breaches than others. To do this:

- *Specify character set.* For every response containing HTML content, the application should include within the `Content-Type` header a directive specifying a standard recognized character set; for example, `charset=ISO-8859-1`. As a double check to this recommendation:

    a. Ensure the user interface does not show navigation to unauthorized functions.

    b. Ensure server-side authentication or authorization checks are not missing.

- *Test with various privilege roles.* Using a proxy, browse an application with a privileged role. Then, retest using a less privileged role. If the server responses are alike, there are probably vulnerabilities. Some testing proxies directly support this type of analysis.

- *Test access control by privilege.* To verify that the authorization works, directly test the logic of access control implementation in the code by logically following a single privileged request through the code.

Session Fixation

Risk level: **HIGH**

Session fixation permits an attacker to hijack a valid user session by changing a session ID. In computer network security, session fixation attacks attempt to exploit the vulnerability of a system that allows one user to fixate (set) another user's session identifier (SID). Most session fixation attacks rely on SIDs being accepted from URLs (query string) or from POST data.

Prudent countermeasures that can be taken include:

- *Avoid transmission of SIDs.* A web site should be prevented from receiving SIDs in GET/POST variables contained within URLs.

- *Delete the old SID and create a new SID.* When authenticating a user, a web application must delete any and all previous SID numbers and assign a new SID for each new session.

Insecure Cookies

Risk level: **MEDIUM**

Since cookies have parameters that can be set, it is relatively easy for a developer to choose security-healthy options. In this case, the parameters deal with a "secure flag" option and choosing a browser that automatically includes encryption. The following sections describe remediations for five cookie vulnerabilities that we too often see during audits.

Cookies with No Secure Flag

Risk level: **MEDIUM**

The simple way to solve this problem is to enforce that the Secure flag is set for all cookies and, of course, using HTTPS for all transactions. The Secure flag is an option that can be set by an application server when sending a new cookie to the user within an HTTP response. The purpose of the Secure flag is to prevent cookies from being observed by unauthorized parties due to the transmission of a cookie in clear text.

Cookies Set to Expire in the Distant Future

Risk level: **MEDIUM**

Use the option within cookies to set expiration dates and have cookies expire when the user closes the browser—that is, mark the cookie as "Session only."

Cookies with No HttpOnly Flag

Risk level: **LOW**

Another option within cookies is to set the HTTPOnly flag as "on." If the HttpOnly attribute is set on a cookie, then the cookie's value cannot be read or set by client-side JavaScript. This measure can prevent certain client-side attacks, such as cross-site scripting, from trivially capturing the cookie's value via an injected script.

Cookies Created on the Client Side

Risk level: **LOW**

It is critical in cookie security to ensure that only trusted cookies are used. By default, any cookie or piece of software created by a user is not secure. The primary trusted partner in a relationship between a user and a web application is the web application. Therefore, it is prudent to enforce the creation of server-side cookies only and not allow those cookies created on the client side.

Cookies Scoped to Parent Domain

Risk level: **LOW**

Cookies can be a very good attack point for hackers depending on what is stored in them. Information can be exposed when the appropriate scope or, in this case, the scope of the domains with access to the cookie is not set for cookies. It is important to set stringent restrictions on cookie paths to include only intended directories and ensure that no unintended subdomains are included in the paths.

Weak Input Validation at the Application Level

Risk level: **HIGH**

Since access control is paramount to security, strong validation is required within a web application both for the authentication and validation of input. The recommendations for this general class are the same as those listed earlier in the "Unauthorized Access" section.

Lack of Validated Input Allowing Automatic Script Execution

Risk level: **HIGH**

Any active code that is inserted into a data input field is a security landmine, especially for a field not expecting to receive active code. Input fields need to be stringently filtered to keep out unwanted active code. To ensure that active code is restricted:

- *Validate all user input.* All user input must be validated before being written to the database. Validation should occur within the server application because client-side validation cannot be trusted.

- *Discard and report nonconforming text.* Upon any deviation from the required text pattern (e.g., an unusual e-mail address pattern, nonalphabetic characters for first or last names), all filtered-out text should be reported as an error to the user and discarded from further processing. It is also prudent to keep a log of discarded text transactions for security analysis.

Unauthorized Access by Parameter Manipulation

Risk level: **HIGH**

Hackers gaining unauthorized access to sensitive data is another example of why building security into the design for hiding and restricting access is so important for web application planning. In this case, malicious users change data or lever what they would otherwise not see toward building an attack. To restrict access:

- *Authenticate all user queries.* All query information should be verified and authorized on the web server before being allowed to access any data. The validation actions include associating the requested information with the authenticated user, such as by verifying that there is a connection between the user account and the user name. For clarity, a parameter manipulation attack compromises weak protection and bad application design in order to act upon data residing in a user browser that would otherwise be invisible and unable to be changed by a user. The data can be session tokens, values stored in cookies, HTTP headers, or even prices in web carts.

- *Reject and alert on unauthorized requests.* Any unauthorized requests should be rejected and an alert should be sent to the system administrator for further investigation. It is also prudent to keep a log of rejected request transactions for security analysis.

Buffer Overflows

Risk level: **HIGH**

Since buffer overflows can result in hackers gaining access to otherwise unauthorized data, it is important to take the following proactive measures to make sure they are never allowed to occur:

- *Test for and identify buffer overflow vulnerabilities.* Do this by entering large values into the form-input and header and cookie fields. Look for a lack of filtering or outright rejection of inappropriate data.

- *Enforce the length of all input fields.* You should ensure that input fields do not allow arbitrary amounts of data by filtering or disallowing any data beyond the absolute-maximum number of expected characters.

Form Submitted Using the GET Method

Risk level: **HIGH**

There are more secure HTTP methods of retrieving and submitting data than the GET method, so in a nutshell don't use it. Instead, use the POST method. All forms and user input can be submitted with it, and it will embed the submitted information in the HTTP body and not in its header. This will ensure the data is encrypted when using HTTPS.

Redirects and Forwards to Insecure Sites

Risk level: **LOW-MEDIUM**

Since sending a browser session to a surprise or unexpected web site can lead to a security breach for the user, it is essential to put into place mitigation steps to ensure unintended redirects and forwards simply do not happen. In order to set them up:

- *Don't use redirect parameters*. If destination parameters can't be avoided, then ensure that supplied values are validated and that they are authorized for the user only. Also ensure that unknown, potentially dangerous URL values cannot be input.

- *Use only mapped values, not the actual URL*. If destination parameters must be used, they should be mapped values rather than the actual destination URL. Server-side code should translate this mapping value to the target URL.

- *Forward or redirect table*. Wherever possible, create an updateable forward or redirect table that the application will send inquiries to in order to source valid URLs.

- *Test for unintended or broken redirects*. Do this by spidering the web application to see if it generates any redirects (HTTP response codes 300–7, typically 302). Look at the parameters supplied prior to the redirect to see if they appear to be a target URL or a piece of such a URL. If so, change the URL target and observe whether the site redirects to the new target.

Application Susceptible to Brute-Force Attacks

Risk level: **LOW**

It is imperative to protect input fields, particularly authentication fields, from a malicious user who simply enters data over and over again in an attempt to gain information or to compromise security. To set up protection:

- *Lock and suspend the account.* Implement account locking or temporary account suspension for any user account that incurs more than five unsuccessful login attempts in a short period of time (typically no more than three minutes of elapsed time should be allowed).

- *Set a time period for locking.* Locking an account for a period of ten to fifteen minutes is a realistic deterrent to foil brute-force attackers; another option to consider is requiring account unlocking by an administrator.

Client-Side Enforcement of Server-Side Security

Risk level: **MEDIUM**

Enforce server-side testing for all validation and then perform testing to ensure that only server-side validation is permissible. Ensure any security checks that are performed on the client side are duplicated or validated on the server side.

Injection Flaws

Risk level: **HIGH**

Since injection flaws allow attackers to relay malicious code from a web application to another system, they may attack other web sites, operating systems, and databases. Five specific types of injection flaws are described in subsequent sections. The key countermeasures that can be taken include filtering every input field, denying absolutely every surprise or untrusted character, and validating users, perhaps several times, prior to giving them the access they request.

- **Filtering and rejecting**: All data other than expected data, such as expected size, type, and character type, should be rejected by the web application immediately. It may not always be practical, but it is advisable to create an alert for any rejected data for further investigation. It is also prudent to keep a log of data rejects for security analysis.

- **Dynamic SQL queries**: Wherever possible, do not use dynamic SQL queries; instead use parameterized SQL queries. For clarity, a dynamic SQL query is an SQL query built at runtime. It is used to dynamically set values or filters on the fly. Dynamic SQL queries are the bane of SQL injection attacks. There are safer SQL queries that are predefined and in which placeholders are used for parameters; the parameter values are supplied at execution time. The most important reason to use parameterized queries is to avoid SQL injection attacks.

- **Safe API**: Utilize a safe API (application programming interface) that avoids the use of an interpreter entirely or provides a parameterized interface. Even apparently safe APIs, such as stored procedures that are parameterized, may still be susceptible to SQL injection. If a parameterized API is not available, input should be strongly filtered to remove escaped syntax and escape characters. For clarity, an API is a set of prebuilt routines and tools designed to allow external communications with an application in an automated or semiautomated fashion. A good API makes it easier and faster to develop a program by providing all the building blocks, and all programs using a common API will have similar interfaces. This makes it easier for programmers to connect various applications.

- **White list**: Positive or "white list" input validation is recommended, but it is not a complete defense, as many applications require special characters in their input.

- **Test code logic**: Test code logic to see if the application uses interpreters safely. Code analysis tools can help a security analyst find the use of interpreters and trace the data flow through the application. Vulnerability testers can confirm the existence of vulnerabilities.

- **Automated dynamic scanning and manual testing**: To test for SQL injection vulnerabilities, use automated dynamic scanning, which exercises the application and may provide insight into whether exploitable injection flaws exist. It is also recommended that you employ manual vulnerability testing.

SQL Injection

Risk level: **HIGH**

A subset of injection vulnerabilities, SQL injection vulnerabilities are very severe and can result in a database being read, changed, and made unavailable. It is critical to invoke countermeasures; by default, give the lowest-possible privileges to any party trying to communicate with the database or its server by doing the following:

- *Use dynamic SQL queries.* Use parameterized SQL Queries and avoid the use of dynamic SQL queries.

- *Enforce access permissions with the fewest possible privileges.* Give users access to only those files, programs, and data that are necessary for business use. Every other resource is off limits. The best way to implement least-privilege permissions is to, by default, make all resources unavailable to users and then add privileges as exceptions to the default.

- *Validate user input with a white list comparison.* White lists are lists of acceptable characters, words or strings, names, and other welcomed data. All input other than that on the white list should be disregarded.

- *Strip user input of special characters.* Also validate that input before using it directly in SQL queries.

- *Check input for appropriate/expected length.* Filter out strings or words that exceed expected and desired length of input. For instance, you might indicate that a state or province name in North America should not exceed the amount of characters in "Massachusetts."

- *Ensure that SQL does not process user commands.*

- *Apply default error handling.* Ensure that all error messages do not reveal any details about users or about how the web application environment operates. Instead, give error numbers to error messages referring users to on an identified help line. If something unexpected happens, error conditions should default to one safe state, which can, again, have a message to call a help line.

- *Implement logical security for databases.* This should involve specifying users, roles, and permissions at the database layer.

- *Perform SQL testing.* Conduct regular vulnerability testing and code testing for potential SQL injection vulnerabilities.

- *Also apply to XML databases and other types of databases.* Other types of databases can also have similar problems with XPath and XQuery injections. The previous recommendations can similarly be applied to any programming language with any type of database. For clarity, extensible markup language (XML) is a language used by web site developers to create and display web pages. An XML database allows XML data to be stored and retrieved while remaining in the XML format.

Blind SQL Injection

Risk level: **HIGH**

As explained in Chapter 3, a blind SQL injection attack is a form of SQL injection. This type of attack is just as dangerous as a regular SQL injection and should be dealt with in the same way. Refer to the recommendations in the preceding section.

Link Injection

Risk level: **HIGH**

Since a link injection attack usually results in the defacement of a web page, this type of attack can cause damage to reputation and financial loss. To address this vulnerability, enforce strong filtering at input fields with attention to stopping all control characters. The following table lists the various control characters.

Characters	Descriptions
|	(pipe)
&amp;	(ampersand)
;	(semicolon)
$	(dollar sign)
%	(percent sign)
@	(at sign)
'	(single apostrophe)
"	(quotation mark)
\'	(backslash-escaped apostrophe)
\"	(backslash-escaped quotation mark)
< and >	(triangular parentheses)
()	(parentheses)
+	(plus sign)
CR	(carriage return, ASCII 0x0d)
LF	(line feed, ASCII 0x0a)

HTTP Header Injection Vulnerability

Risk level: **HIGH**

Since header injection vulnerabilities are caused by insufficient filtering during the creation of on-the-fly HTTP headers, and this code attacks a program at the host, take the following countermeasures for this vulnerability:

- *Filter user input.* Ensure that stringent filtering is done particularly on user input, where the input may be then used in an HTTP header response.

- *Harden host programs.* Verify that all programs, particularly interpreters, are minimally susceptible to untrusted data by separating untrusted data before it reaches programs. An interpreter is a program that is used to convert the high-level language commands into machine-readable binary language in a line-by-line fashion in near real-time. Each time an interpreter gets a high-level language code to be executed, it converts the code into an intermediate code before converting it into the machine code. Each part of the code is interpreted and then executed separately in a sequence.

HTTP Response-Splitting Attack

Risk level: **HIGH**

HTTP response-splitting is a type of attack where a hacker sends malicious data to a vulnerable application, which the application then displays in an HTTP response header. An HTTP response header contains detailed information about an HTTP Sent or Received message. These headers are typically never seen by an average user but are quite available to view on a browser. This is done simply by using the appropriate command or getting the appropriate viewing tool for any web browser. Since the response header can be viewed by a potential hacker, it is recommended that an application be set to avoid copying user-controllable data into any HTTP response header. If this is unavoidable, then the data should be strictly validated to prevent header injection attacks. In most situations, it will be appropriate to allow only short alphanumeric strings to be copied into headers, and any other input should be rejected.

The following countermeasures need to be taken to avoid this type of attack:

- *Do not allow CR or LF characters into an application.* Prevent an application from accepting input that contains CR (carriage return) or LF (line feed) in an HTTP header.

- *Harden the application.* An application should not be vulnerable to the injection of CR or LF characters.

Unauthorized View of Data

Risk level: **LOW-HIGH**

Restrict all views to data as "No access by default," and then allow intentional views to only authorized, carefully authenticated personnel and users.

Under this vulnerability class, there are ten subclasses, which are similar in that they all reveal unnecessary and potentially risky information. Each subclass is addressed in the following sections.

The following countermeasures can be taken to protect against the unauthorized view of data:

- *Restrict direct object references by default.* Do not allow insecure direct object references for protecting each object that is accessible by users (e.g., object number, file name). This can be done by using indirect references and verifying access authority for each user.

- *Prevent unauthorized access to objects.* Implement indirect object references per user or session, which prevents unauthorized access to objects. For example, instead of using an object's actual name, replace names of authorized objects with a drop-down list of resource numbers authorized for each user. This requires the application to map the per-user indirect reference back to the actual object.

- *Validate access authorization to objects.* Whenever users want to gain direct access to an important object, such as a file or an important section of an application like money transfer, they should be forced to reauthenticate and then their identification should be double-checked against an authorization list for that object.

- *Limit mapping.* For both direct and indirect references, ensure that the mapping to the direct reference limits access to objects authorized for each user.

- *Review manual code.* Manually perform a code review of the application to verify whether direct and indirect reference logic is implemented securely.

Web Application Source Code Disclosed

Risk Level: **LOW**

Source code is something that an unauthorized person should never see, as it can reveal how an application works. With this knowledge in hand, a hacker can intelligently look for vulnerabilities and subsequently mount an attack. The following are basic steps you can take to avoid disclosing source code or pieces of source code:

- *Keep patches up to date.* Ensure all system patches related to source code disclosure are installed. It is important to ensure that patch upgrades are up to date. Although this may be a simple concept, it is often difficult to achieve in an enterprise environment.

- *Do not leave application source code in HTML comments.* This step requires quality control testing to search all related HTML, plus whatever other web application programming languages are used, to find and delete all comments and fragments of comments.

- *Separate development, testing, and production.* Remove all source code files from the production environment. Ideally, development, testing, and production environments are completely separate. This separation includes both physical devices and personnel responsible for each environment.

Web Directories Enumerated

Risk level: **LOW**

Unauthorized viewing of data includes the scope of the naming convention of files. A hacker can identify naming conventions to assist in making further inquiries into the structure of an environment and subsequently mount an attack. The countermeasure taken is similar as that described in the "Unauthorized View of Data" section, but in this case the issue addressed is hiding directory names. To do so:

- *Enforce naming convention to disguise the actual names of all directories, devices, and services where possible.* This will ensure the names do not reveal their function.

- *Do not use theme names for naming objects.* Theme names would be ones like "Star Trek" or "X-Men." Implement a naming convention that hampers name guessing of other objects even if a malicious user gains possession of one valid object name.

Active Directory Object Default Page on Server

Risk level: **LOW**

Unnecessary disclosure of how the Active Directory manages objects is a potential security threat, as it provides insight into how the files and other objects within the directory are stored. This information could be used to create an attack. To prevent this from happening:

- *Deny unnecessary access.* Deny access to and remove any pages that are not part of the application being hosted on the web server.

- *Enforce access controls for unrelated pages.* If web application users require access to any unrelated pages, user authentication and access control for these pages should be strictly enforced.

- *Produce logs and alerts for failed access attempts.* Too-many failed access attempts to unrelated pages should be logged and alerts should be generated. This is prudent for the purpose of security analysis.

- *Deny default access.* Access to unrelated pages should be granted on a restricted basis.

Temporary Files Left in the Environment

Risk level: **LOW**

Temporary files are useful tools for developers when they are creating programs. They should never be seen by anyone other than the developers, as they provide insight as to how the programming functions. In the hands of a hacker, this information provides leverage to mount an attack. To guarantee that no temporary files remain:

- *Remove temporary files.* Remove test/temporary or backup scripts/files on the web application server.

- *Remove unnecessary files and scripts.* Ensure there are no other scripts/files on the server that are not essential for its normal operation.

- *Test access controls.* Ensure that testing/temporary files and backup scripts/files can be accessed only by parties with the appropriate privileges.

Internal IP Address Revealed by Web Server

Risk level: **MEDIUM**

It is never necessary to reveal to the outside world or to users actual internal IP addresses. It is best to obfuscate them in the following ways:

- *Implement network address translation (NAT).* Doing so provides internal IP addresses with aliases or pretend names, allowing users on the Internet to access these addresses on the corporate network. This process is accomplished with the use of an intermediate server, a list of valid IP addresses, and a comparable list of alias addresses for use with the outside world.

- *Do not reveal IP addresses to any user.* And certainly do not reveal internal IP addresses associated with any services or devices, including the web server software platform.

Server Path Disclosed

Risk level: **MEDIUM**

Similarly to not revealing internal IP addresses to the outside world, it is important not to reveal to any user or the outside world the actual paths for any servers. To conceal them:

- *Set customErrors mode attribute value to "On RemoteOnly."* This way, should an error message be generated with regard to a server path, it will be generic and not reveal any details in the ASP.NET environment. Similar selections of nonrevealing error messages should be implemented in all other programming environments.

- *Create a custom error page for users.* The page should only display generic messages, such as "An error has occurred. Please contact the system administrator."

- *Eliminate errors with patches.* If an error message is caused by a problem that can be fixed with a security patch, then download the relevant security patch depending on the issue existing on your web server or web application.

Hidden Directory Detected

Risk level: **LOW**

A hidden directory is a directory that is not displayed by default. I often used a hidden directory or folder of files for storing user preferences and for preserving the status of various tools. Hidden directories should not be able to be viewed other than by authorized administrative, operations, and development personnel. In the hands of a person with malicious intent, the information stored in hidden directory files can be used to mount an attack.

To reduce the risk, issue a "404—Not Found" response status code instead of a "403—Forbidden" status code when a user attempts to access a directory they are not authorized to view. This change will obfuscate the presence of directories on the site and will reduce the chance of exposing the site structure.

Unencrypted VIEWSTATE

Risk level: **HIGH**

Since VIEWSTATE is a source of temporary storage that allows ASP.NET users to store all the temporary information about a web page, it might contain personal information and is definitely confidential. It should never be allowed to fall into the hands of an unauthorized person. ASP.NET is a Microsoft-created set of web application development tools. The benefit for developers is they can create dynamic web sites while using a visual command interface.

Always encrypt the VIEWSTATE. For clarity, the VIEWSTATE is a source of temporary storage that allows ASP.NET users to store all the temporary information about a web page, such as which panels are open and in use, the options that are currently chosen, the current data in each text box, and other information.

Obsolete Web Server

Risk level: **MEDIUM**

Obsolete software needs to be replaced because security patches are no longer installed to keep it secure. This possibly commits a double omission: a) obsolete software, and therefore possibly also obsolete hardware, should be replaced with technology that is fully secure with up-to-date patches and revisions; and b) unnecessary disclosure of technology details, particularly technology with known vulnerabilities, is simply asking for trouble.

To resolve this:

- *Update the version of the server you are using.* Update your server to the most recent version of the web site platform.

- *Keep your patching up to date.*

- *Hide technology identifiers.* Eliminate all unnecessary announcements of hardware and software to electronic scanning and electronic inquiries.

Query Parameter in SSL Request

Risk level: **MEDIUM**

This vulnerability is very similar to the ones previously discussed in the "Information Submitted Using the GET Method" section. As with the vulnerabilities described there, you counter this one by using the POST method.

Error Handling

Risk level: **HIGH**

When identifying errors to users, an application should not inadvertently reveal overly informative details about how the application functions. All errors must be remediated as per a formal change management process. To prevent the application from disclosing too much information:

- *Create unified and nonrevealing error messages.* The application should output generic error messages (for example, "An unexpected error occurred. Please contact the system administrator.").

- *Produce logs and alerts.* All error messages should be handled and logged (to the system's event log or database) and the application owner alerted.

- *After identifying the cause, remediate.* Once an alert has been sent, there should be a policy in place to enforce that the application owner determines its cause and applies the appropriate fix.

- *Implement a formal ticket resolution process.* These and all other security alerts should be input into a trouble-ticket procedure with a formal closing process for each ticket.

Cross-Site Scripting Attacks

Risk level: **HIGH**

The countermeasures for the injection-like attacks performed by cross-site scripting (XSS) attacks constitute a superset of approaches similar to those used for SQL injection attacks. By default, give the lowest-possible privileges to any party trying to communicate with the database or its server.

See the earlier "SQL Injection" section for recommendations that also apply here. In addition to those, consider the following:

- *Specify HTML coding.* Specify an HTML encoding mechanism for all HTML output from browsers, such as UTF-8.

- *Strongly filter/sanitize data.* This applies to data being sent from the application to browsers and from the browsers to the web application.

- *Provide security-awareness training.* The training should constantly reinforce the idea of not responding to any e-mail, instant messaging, third-party web site, or phone call requesting users to provide their credentials or personal information.

Reflected Cross-Site Scripting Attack

Risk level: **HIGH**

In most situations where user-controllable data is copied into application responses, XSS attacks can be prevented by using layers of defense as follows:

- *Strongly validate input.* When doing so, give specific attention to the type of content that it is expected to contain. For example, personal names should consist of alphabetical and a small range of typographical characters and be relatively short; a year of birth should consist of exactly four numerals; and e-mail addresses should match a well-defined regular expression.

- *Reject input that fails validation.* Input that fails the validation should be rejected, not sanitized.

- *Perform HTML-encoding for user input.* User input should be HTML-encoded at any point where it is copied into application responses. All HTML metacharacters, including < >,",', and =, should be replaced with the corresponding HTML entities (< > so so forth)

- *Remove control characters.* In all cases, all user input fields should be parsed to remove the characters in the following chart.

Characters	Descriptions
|	(pipe)
&amp;	(ampersand)
;	(semicolon)
$	(dollar sign)
%	(percent sign)
@	(at sign)
'	(single apostrophe)
"	(quotation mark)
\'	(backslash-escaped apostrophe)
\"	(backslash-escaped quotation mark)
< and >	(triangular parentheses)
()	(parentheses)
+	(plus sign)
CR	(carriage return, ASCII 0x0d)
LF	(line feed, ASCII 0x0a)

- *Filter for dangerous syntax.* In cases where the application's functionality allows users to author content using a restricted subset of HTML tags and attributes (for example, blog comments that allow limited formatting and linking), parse the supplied HTML to validate that it does not use any dangerous syntax.

Stored Cross-Site Scripting Attack

Risk level: **HIGH**

Since the storage of XSS is the most dangerous attack in this class and is caused by web applications that store user data within a web site page for later use, it is extremely important for data to be stringently filtered at input and to understand exactly how data is stored within a web site page. If the data is malicious, it can be passed onto successive visitors to the page, so employ the following countermeasures:

- *Do a vulnerability test of HTML code and JavaScript content.* A test of how all input data is stored should be done prior to moving code into production.

- *Test out-of-band communications channels.* Also do a vulnerability test and analysis of precisely how any user input data is received and stored via out-of-band channels. Out-of-band channels, in this case, refer to any other mechanism besides the expected user input fields.

- *Have administrators test and identify user data.* A testing process must be established for all areas of a web application accessible by administrators in order to identify the presence of user data in these otherwise-"restricted" areas of the application.

- *XSS-reflected recommendations.* In addition, implement all the recommendations in the "Cross-Site Scripting Reflected Attack" section.

Cross-Site Request Forgery Attack

Risk level: **HIGH**

Preventing cross-site request forgery (CSRF) usually requires the inclusion of an unpredictable token in each HTTP request. Such tokens should, at a minimum, be unique per user session. The preferred option is to include the unique token in a hidden field. This causes the value to be sent in the body of the HTTP request, avoiding its inclusion in the URL, which is more prone to exposure.

The unique token can also be included in the URL itself or in a URL parameter. However, such placement runs a greater risk that the URL will be exposed to an attacker, thus compromising the secret token. The CSRF Guard available at the Open Web Application Security Project (OWASP) can automatically include such tokens in Java EE, .NET, or PHP apps (see `www.owasp.org/index.php/Category:OWASP_CSRFGuard_Project`). OWASP's Enterprise Security API Project (ESAPI) includes methods developers can use to prevent CSRF vulnerabilities (see `www.owasp.org/index.php/Category:OWASP_Enterprise_Security_API`).

OWASP is a worldwide application-security organization based in Australia that provides educational material about web application security for free to anyone. ESAPI is a free, open-source library offering web application security controls that makes it easier for programmers to write lower-risk applications.

Java, created by Sun Microsystems, is a high-level programming language that is created for use by developers writing Internet-based applications. Java EE is the Java Enterprise Edition.

Scripting languages are high-level programming languages that were developed primarily to assist web application developers in creating dynamic HTML content. Dynamic content changes each time it is viewed. For instance, it may show the time of day, the profile of the viewer, or the geographic location of the viewer or it may add functionality such as creating graphic displays and creating different menu styles. These languages, such as JavaScript, ASP, Python, Perl, PHP, and JSP, are interpreted at runtime, which is why they can dynamically present data.

Another measure to take is to require users to reauthenticate to renew the proof that they are a valid user. This is a commonly used security methodology, which can be seen, for instance, on the Amazon site when moving from the phase of selecting items to the phase of paying for items. At the beginning of the payment phase, the user is asked to reauthenticate.

Security Misconfigurations and Using Known Vulnerable Components

Risk level: **MEDIUM**

Wherever cost effective, it is best to replace legacy technology, which is no longer supported with security updates, with more recent technology that is well supported with security updates.

Most component vendors do not create vulnerability patches for old versions. Instead, they simply fix the problem in the next version. Be sure to ensure that patches and upgrades for the most secure recent versions are done in accordance with a corporate security policy. This can be done in the following ways:

- *Document legacy components in a library*. Identify all components and their versions in the corporate software library, including all dependencies.

- *Keep informed of legacy component security issues*. Monitor the security of these components in public databases, project mailing lists, and security mailing lists, and keep them up to date.

- *Establish security policies for legacy technology*. Set security policies governing component use, such as requiring certain software development practices, passing security tests, and outlining acceptable licenses.

- *Add security wrappers*. Where possible, add security wrappers around components to disable unused functionality and/or secure weak or vulnerable aspects of the component.

Denial-of-Service Attack

Risk level: **HIGH**

These high-profile attacks should be dealt with up front by providing countermeasures and monitoring as follows:

- *Stabilize high-volume traffic flow*. Ensure that the application functions properly when presented with large volumes of transactions, requests, or traffic.

- *Monitor event logs*. Monitor the event logs of application servers, firewalls, intrusion detection systems (IDS), and intrusion prevention systems (IPS), and set thresholds to alert for anomalous traffic increases that are indicative of a DoS attack.

- *Block originating IP addresses.* Once you have determined the originating IP address or addresses of the attack, block them either at the firewall level (to kill HTTP requests) or further upstream at the ISP level (to kill network-level floods).

- *Prevent ICMP floods.* Implement technology to identify and prevent ICMP (Internet Control Message Protocol) flood attacks.

- *Block repeated requests from a single URL.* Large-volume requests from a single URL usually mean malicious activity, as a normal activity pattern would consist of a solo or low volume of requests from a single URL.

- *Implement an intrusion prevention system.* Route traffic through an intrusion prevention system (IPS) to actively detect and block DoS and DDoS attacks.

- *Implement a third-party denial of service (DoS)/distributed denial of service (DDoS) prevention service.* Consider setting up one of these services, which may include the use of proxy servers to scrub attacks and load multiple instances of the application server for alternate routing.

Related Security Issues

Risk level: **HIGH**

Data at rest, such as in storage, needs to be secured equally to data in motion, such as data flowing between a web application server and a user's browser. Securing data at rest can be done through:

- **Encryption**: Encrypt web application logs, keys, certificates, passwords, and all other sensitive or confidential information.

- **Hiding and restricting access**: Remove sensitive files (etc/passwd) from production or restrict file access to only authorized personnel.

- **Backing up to secure location**: Do not back up web application source code to the web server; instead use a more secure location.

Storage of Data at Rest

Risk level: **HIGH**

Data encryption and data masking are both recommended for protecting data at rest. Data masking is used to obfuscate data so that it typically cannot be seen by developers and database testers, who have no business reasons to view private or confidential data. In their cases, the data is present but hidden. One of the best forms of protecting data at rest, of course, is to limit access to it on a business need basis.

There are many different methodologies of data access control, all of which are designed for different environments. For instance, discretionary access controls (DACs) are controls placed on data by the data owner. The owner decides who has what privileges and access to data. DACs are commonly used. Mandatory access controls (MACs) are control systems used in more highly sensitive environments where controls are determined by both the owner and by the system. The system is instructed to provide access controls based on the clearance level of a user and the classification of the data to be accessed. Another example is the role-based access control system, in which access is granted based on the functions that a user is allowed to perform. The most applicable methodology or version of various methodologies should be chosen to meet an organization's specific needs.

Timely destruction of data is another important element for security of data at rest. Increasingly, large amounts of useless data have become a target for a security breach. There should be stringent policies in place for data life cycle management, which includes the timely, secure destruction of data.

Storage of Account Lists

Risk level: **HIGH**

A major part of security 101 is managing the life cycles of accounts and account lists. Prevent users from gaining access to a list of account names. If a user list must be presented, then use only pseudonyms (screen names) that map to the actual account list.

When setting up account life cycle management:

- *Disable stale accounts.* On a periodic basis, review all system accounts and disable all accounts that cannot be associated with a business process and owner.

- *Ensure that all accounts have an expiration date.* This is a fallback protective measure against stale accounts staying in existence by default. In the worst-case situation where a valid account is automatically expired, the user will complain to the help desk, and the help desk will investigate and reinstate a valid account.

- *Create a daily report of account life cycle policy violations.* Create an automated daily report that is sent to a senior IT administrator which identifies: locked-out accounts, disabled accounts, accounts with passwords that exceed the maximum password age, and accounts that appear dormant.

- *Disable accounts immediately upon termination of an employee or contractor.*

When setting up secure long-term storage:

- *Secure storage after disabling accounts.* When a dormant account is disabled, any files associated with that account should be encrypted and moved to a secure file server for analysis of whether the data should be retained or destroyed by security or management personnel.

When managing access control:

- *Create strong passwords for admin accounts.* Require that all nonadministrator accounts have strong passwords that contain letters, numbers, and special characters; are changed at least every 90 days; and are not allowed to use the previous 15 passwords as a new password. These values can be adjusted based on the specific business needs of the organization.

- *Use and configure account lockouts for failed logins.* After a set number of failed login attempts, the account should be locked for a standard period of time.

- *Monitor failed logins.* Monitor event logs and set up alerts for unusual activities, such as attempts to access deactivated accounts and failed login attempts.

- *Flag anomalous behavior.* Profile users' typical account usage and flag anomalous usage.

Password Storage

Risk level: **HIGH**

Managing the life cycle and storage of passwords is absolutely critical to security since passwords are fundamental to authentication and access control. To protect passwords:

- *Store passwords in hashed form.* This will protect them from exposure regardless of where they are stored. Hashed form is also less susceptible to being reversed than encrypted data.

- *Avoid hardcoding passwords.* Passwords should never be hardcoded in any source code. Be sure to never store unencrypted passwords anywhere, including within databases, cookies, or text files.

- *Strongly protect encryption keys.* If encryption is used for password protection, then the decryption keys must be strongly protected.

- *Securely store or destroy artifacts.* Ensure artifacts containing passwords, such as logs, dumps, and backups, are securely stored or securely destroyed.

Insufficient Patch Management

Risk level: **HIGH**

Insufficient patch management is one of the most common causes for security breaches, and so stringent patch management is a security must. Ensure patching is kept up to date for all software platforms within a web application environment, but only after patches are tested in a nonproduction environment.

Summary

Prevention is the best form of remediation and there are a number of key preventative takeaways to reduce the need for excessive remediations that we have covered in this chapter:

- Implement strong security during the development phase of a web application.

- Replace obsolete technology with security-supported new technology.

- Do not implement technology with known security flaws.

- Implement strong authentication, then enforce it continuously and test it regularly.

- Enforce access privileges on a need-to-know basis only. Make the denial of access the default and then provide access only on a need-to-read basis.

- Manage the life cycles of passwords and accounts.

- Manage the life cycle of sessions and session IDs.

- Filter, filter, filter all data input fields. Reject everything unexpected.

- Filter or parse data flowing from an application to browsers to mitigate cross-site scripting.

- Encrypt any data in motion or data at rest that is sensitive.

- Hash or one-way encrypt all passwords. This includes both passwords in motion and passwords being stored.

- Keep security patching up to date.

- Monitor and identify unusual traffic patterns, especially from unknown IP addresses.

- Log all security activity, both normal and infractions, for analysis and planning.

- Create an event log of unusual traffic patterns and repetitive security events. Create alerts for all serious security infractions.

- Regularly test security for the presence of known vulnerabilities.

CHAPTER 5

How to Build Preventative Countermeasures for Web Application Vulnerabilities

Most of the vulnerabilities identified in Chapter 3 could have been simply avoided by not allowing them to occur in the first place. The best way to avoid creating vulnerabilities in web applications is to plan and build security as part of the development cycle.

Since application-security planning is not a widely understood art, and since it involves time and expenses, it is often neglected. The unfavorable alternative is to test applications for vulnerabilities after they are created in test or beta test mode. As we saw in Chapter 3, this is simply too late.

This issue becomes a decision point for the financial manager responsible for the overall life cycle cost of an application. The decision has many variables:

- including security as intrinsic to the software development life cycle

- the cost of developers' time and expenses

- the cost of hiring external expertise for the process

- the overall least-probable cost, including both the software development life cycle and the estimated costs of security breaches

- determining the importance of taking reasonable steps with regard to governance, risk management, and compliance (GRC)

Real-life examples of vulnerabilities that auditors find during business in the course of usual activities are identified in Chapter 3. The reality of how security teams in the field address these vulnerabilities is found in Chapter 4. The results of what happens when the vulnerabilities are found and compromised by malicious third parties are often shouted out by the media:

- stolen credit card information

- stolen personal information being used for fraud

- stolen money

- denial of service attacks; preventing service

- stolen sensitive information compromising business and national security

- web site defacements

The costs to the victims are:

- damage to reputation

- financial losses due to lost business, production, clients, and partners

- damage to clients

- compliance-violation expenses

- legal expenses

- money spent on emergency-security countermeasures

- public relations fees

The cost of prevention therefore needs to be analyzed in terms of its alternative scenario, which indeed may include the occurrence of episodes from the "scary list" just outlined. Prevention is the preferred method of vulnerability management, and it can be built intrinsically into a web application. The formal methodology for doing so is called the security-in-software-development life cycle (S-SDLC).

Once an application is put into production, the change management portion of S-SDLC should be stringently enforced. For example, one of the most widely found sources of application-security vulnerabilities is failing to implement security-related patches and revisions in a timely fashion. This is a human error associated with change management that should be a carefully documented and enforced core to security policy.

Security-in-Software-Development Life Cycle

Embedding security should be done at every phase of software development, including code writing, change management, and testing during and after development. The key components of building strong security into the SDLC process are:

- **Business requirements**: These requirements must be identified in sufficient detail and clarity so that the application design phase can proceed efficiently.

- **Security requirements**: Right alongside the business requirements, it is important to define all security requirements from a business perspective.

- **Threat modelling:** Somewhere early in the security design phase, threat modelling should be done in order to identify the potential threats that exist specific to the application. For instance, it would be a waste of money to have controls for theft protection when there is nothing to steal. Threat modelling might also assist in identifying the threats from potential vulnerabilities and the controls available to mitigate the associated risk.

- **Design:** The design phase involves translating the business requirements into architecture and determining how the applications will function. The design specification should address how security functions will be incorporated and should highlight all major security concerns and how they will be managed.

- **A policy for secure web application code:** Writing secure code occurs only by adhering to a writing a policy or framework for doing so. The framework should include technical processes for writing securely for every coding language, interim testing, separation of duties for code writers and testers, implementing controls for all known vulnerabilities identified during threat modelling, end user testing and remediation, implementing backups and backup revision cataloguing, and so on.

- **A framework for secure web application code:** Although mentioned in the previous paragraph, this topic requires further attention. There are open-source guides available from educational resources such as OWASP with detailed recommendations as to how to write code that minimizes the chances of creating vulnerabilities. There are also training courses available on the topic. I recommend that financial executives give consideration to ensuring that their development team is sufficiently trained in the art of writing secure code and that management enforces policy regarding writing secure code. There are more details about this topic in the section "Framework for Secure Web Application Code."

- **A separation between code and production environment:** Development code should be written on a server that is separate and isolated from any production technology. This is typically called a development environment. To fully describe the process, at the risk of jumping ahead, once development is complete and the application is ready to be integrated into the production environment, it is best to move it to a test server. The test server will not provide production services to end users but will be used to stringently test all security throughout the entire integration of devices.

- **Code testing and web application security testing**: There are several methods and technologies for testing code, all of which are discussed in the section "Web Application Security Testing." In addition to testing code, there are tools and methodologies for testing code as it is running, all of which are also discussed in this section. Although I mention testing prior to integration and validation, the idea behind testing is: Always be testing. Testing needs to be done during development but also during integration and validation, preproduction, and continuously during postproduction.

- **Integration and validation**: Most transaction web applications are integrated with other network components such as a back-end database, a proxy server between the web server and the back-end database, other web sites such as payment sites, authentication technology such as multifactor authenticators, back-end administrative services, and of course logical connectivity with users of the web application. All of the devices and services of the web application must be secure within themselves and the communication between all of these technologies must also be strongly secured.

- **Production**: This process involves moving a thoroughly tested application from a test environment into full production and providing the intended business services to end users.

- **Change management**: Web application changes typically are made informally and without vulnerability testing. But without proper controls to test web applications in an environment identical to the production environment as well as the ability to transfer the updates into the production environment, security vulnerabilities may be introduced into the production environment. These vulnerabilities are discussed in more detail in the following section.

Framework for Secure Web Application Code

To mitigate the chances of writing insecure code, several steps should be included in the SDLC, which I will review in this section.

Since writing secure code is fundamental to minimizing the occurrence of vulnerabilities, it is worth elaborating on this topic for the benefit of executives. This step in development is too often overlooked, misunderstood, or deemed to be of secondary importance compared with production deadlines. For executives, it is worth reviewing the basic steps for writing secure code if only to remember that this concept exists and may at some point present an attractive return on investment.

Creating a framework for secure code involves the following aspects:

- **Management buy-in**: Involve executives and other members of management early. Include business process owners, the corporate security committee, and senior financial management from the beginning of the development process, starting with the definition of business requirements for the web application. Get financial commitments from financial management upfront to support the entire security framework. The details of how to engage management are discussed in more detail in Chapter 8.

- **Security team engagement**: Involve the security team from the beginning. Invite the team to the initial planning sessions for any software development to ensure that security is being considered and addressed at all stages of the SDLC, from concept to production. This will help avoid security weaknesses starting right at the inception of the development process.

- **Separation of duties and separation of environments**: In a perfect world, there would exist a separation of all functions relating to security. This includes a separation between coders and testers, a separation between test and production environments, and bringing in only impartial external testers. Unfortunately, due to financial constraints, it is not always possible to attain this level of separation, but it is a useful to get as close as possible to the goal. Some basic considerations include:

  - *Separating development, test, and production systems*: Separate development and quality assurance (QA) environments from the production network.

  - *Separating duties*: Ensure that different people are assigned to do the production coding and the testing of code. Where possible, task different team members for security and for implementation/production.

  - *Using impartial third-party testing*: Use arm's-length third-party testing where applicable, such as for compliance, in cases where internal testers/auditors want the comfort of receiving verification from a third-party tester, or for management, which might want an impartial expert to provide due-diligence testing.

- **Backups**: Include software revision backups, and incorporate an automated revision library for change management of application code.

- **Monitoring and alerts**: This stage involves several steps.

  - *Monitor event logs.* Monitor event logs of all elements of a web application environment including the application, web application platform, operating system(s), hardware platform(s), and firewall.

  - *Create alerts for high-risk activities.* Set up alerts for high-risk activity and create trouble tickets that must be formally closed and regularly reviewed by the appropriate security/end-user committee.

  - *Log application and application-server event logs.* In addition to logging application activity, investigate all high-risk activities, such as exceeded threshold values for failed login attempts and logins during unusual hours.

- **Patching**: It is important to keep patching up to date. Patch all third-party elements of the web application environment in a timely fashion.

- **Authentication and password management**: As described in Chapter 4, managing the password life cycle involves the following five actions.

  - *Ensure password complexity.* Sufficient password complexity minimizes the chance of password guessing or brute-force attacks against passwords.

  - *Regularly change passwords.* Password rotation minimizes the chance of password theft or a user's duplicate password being obtained from another web site.

  - *Reset passwords.* Ensuring that there is a secure mechanism to reset passwords minimizes the chance of stale passwords staying in circulation.

  - *Only store hashed passwords.* You can guarantee that all passwords are kept secure by storing only hashed values and password inputs for users and then comparing the two hashed values.

  - *Use operating system-based access-control facilities.* These mechanisms include operating system permissions and access control lists.

- **Session management**: Chapter 4 also describes how to manage sessions and addresses the following six points.

  - *Token length and randomizing*: Enforce the requirement for users to create sufficiently long and random session token IDs.

  - *Random number generator for session tokens*: Sufficiently secure mechanisms for creating session tokens with a cryptographic random number generator.

  - *Session inactivity timeouts*: To guarantee that inappropriate users don't log on to a session, timeouts should be implemented.

  - *Restrictions on the storage of a session token in cache*: Restrictions need to be set up, as stealing data from cache memory is a favorite hacker activity.

  - *New token for state change*: It is necessary to create secure random tokens, particularly whenever there is a state change.

  - *Limitation of the reuse of tokens*: You should ensure that the token is unique for each user and for each session and you should never allow a session token to be reused in a subsequent session.

- **Secure flags**: The process of setting a secure flag is described in Chapter 4.

- **HttpOnly flag**: Always make sure this flag is set.

- **Indirect file path**: Always display an indirect file path, using the current file as a root for accessing an image. For example, you might use the following code:

  ```
  :\images\pic.jpg
  ```

  instead of the more revealing absolute path

  ```
  C:\programfiles\webapps\project\images\pic.jpg.
  ```

- **SSL or TLS with HTTPS**: For users viewing confidential/sensitive information and for all transactions, implement SSL or TLS with HTTPS.

- **Input validation**: Chapter 4 discusses input validation and filtering content in some detail. Some important aspects include:

  - *Client-side validation*: Implement server side validation versus client-side validation.

  - *Strong input validation*: Implement robust input validation including filtering out all unnecessary control characters.

- **Stringent filtering of rich user content**: This is critically important, requiring that special attention is paid to control characters, any special characters, and the length of responses.

- **Verification of uploaded files**: This can be done in several ways.

  - *Ensure that extension types are as expected.* Parse input file content to ensure it agrees with the file extension type; similarly, ensure that the content of image files agrees with the extension type (.MP3, .jpg).

  - *Guarantee that permitted file size is not exceeded.* Ensure that the size of the files does not exceed that which is expected and allowed.

  - *Filter for permitted character values.* Filter strongly for only allowed values paying special attention to XML and other control characters.

  - *Implement a white list.* The white list should include special files that are not allowed, such as .exe.

- **Output encoding**: Chapter 4 deals with the details of how to encode output safely from a security perspective. Doing so includes:

  - *Encoding output data*: Encode all output that will be returned to an HTML page, being sure to use the appropriate encoding such as that which is HTML or JavaScript specific; avoid sending user data to an operating system.

  - *Using a UTF-8 character set*: Implement a UTF-8 character representation for output in order to preserve the order of translation steps used, which is sometimes critical to the security of the application.

- **Exception and error handling**: Do not reveal user information, authentication information, file names, file paths, or any verbose information. Reveal only the most generic information possible in error messages.

- **Application testing**: There are several necessary components, which follow:

    - *Web application security testing*: Incorporate web application security testing into the SDLC phases, including code planning and code writing. This will be discussed in more detail in the next section.

    - *Testing compliance with policy*: Integrate web application security testing into the security program to evaluate and validate whether the application is operating according to security policy. As part of this step, require authorization for movement into production by both the end user and security personnel.

    - *Known vulnerabilities*: Test applications for all known vulnerabilities.

- **Training**: There are a couple of processes involved in training.

    - *Locate training courses.* Obtain application training courses for developers from organizations such as SANS, CSI, NSI, IEEE, IETF, and CERT.

    - *Set up security for ancillary elements.* Pay attention to security best practices for related topics: database, file management, memory management, and data storage.

Once the application code has been written in a secure fashion, it is of course time to test the code to verify its security health. One might think that after adhering to a framework for writing secure web application code, testing it may be overkill. However, this could not be further from the truth; this is separation of duties in real life. Now on to web application security testing.

Web Application Security Testing

Web application security testing is another topic worth repeating since it takes time and money to execute and does not require additional business functions or add glitz to an application. Since financial executives receive only risk analysis data as the result of testing, they sometimes put this type of testing in the backseat of production priorities.

Web application testing includes:

- **Reviewing lines of code**: Reviewing ensures that lines of code comply with the security plan and that their logic will produce the intended results.

- **Real-time testing**: This type of testing assesses how applications actually respond and function.

- **Constant testing and retesting:** It is necessary to test all the time, including during code writing, after end-user testing, just before introducing the code into production, and continuously thereafter. Testing is especially important after changes are made to the application environment including to both software and network technology.

Manual vs. Automated Code Testing

A source code review is an effective method of detecting security vulnerabilities as well as other logic flaws. Manual reviews, the tried-and-true method of code testing, especially applicable prior to the advent of automated-code testing tools, are time consuming and expensive. The reasons for this include the requirements of:

- **A team effort:** A team effort is necessary since programmers are required to review each other's work. The reasoning for this is that programmers may notice errors in another developer's code with much more clarity than their own errors.

- **Real-time testing:** Reviews need to be repeated at regular intervals to review fresh code or re-review code after recommended changes have been applied.

- **Expertise:** Those reviewing the code need to have extensive application-development experience and security expertise.

However, automated application-source-code analyzer tools can shorten the time and cost required to review and subsequently make the requisite corrections to source code, particularly for large applications. A number of different select tools can analyze source code or a compiled version of the code.

Automated tools are most cost effectively used in the application development environment since correcting security vulnerabilities at an early stage is less expensive than finding and correcting them late in the development cycle. However, automated tools can provide a false sense of security that everything is being addressed, when, in fact, they cannot identify every kind of web application vulnerability and can produce false positives and false negatives. (It should be noted that this also applies to static-code analysis.)

There are two basic models of automated-code testing tools:

- static-code analyzers
- dynamic-code analyzers

Static analyzers collect information based on looking directly at the syntactical structure of code and drawing conclusions about the program's behavior. Dynamic analyzers take a different approach, wherein they evaluate how the code actually behaves when it is interacting with the real world, taking state information into account.

Static-Code Analysis Advantages

Static-code analysis can provide an early security warning system for developers as they write sections of code. A static-code analysis tool:

- *Reduces cost.* This type of analysis greatly reduces the cost of eliminating security defects in software. The earlier an error is detected, the lower the cost of remediation.

- *Finds security vulnerabilities at specific locations.*

- *Is quick and less expensive.* Because this analysis tool is quicker, it is therefore a less expensive means of fixing security vulnerabilities.

- *Provides granularity and scale.* This degree of detail is possible because an automated static-code analysis tool can scan the entire code base rather than just samples of code.

- *Provides immediate feedback.* An analysis tool can be run repetitively, such as after each batch of mitigations is complete.

- *Finds specific classes of problems.* The tool is effective at detecting certain classes of problems that dynamic-code analyzers cannot always find, such as buffer overflows and SQL injection flaws. An alternative solution to using a dynamic-code analyzer is to deploy manual testing by expert testers.

- *Examines how data flows through an application.* In addition to investigating data flows, this tool looks at how specific types of data, such as confidential and personal data, are processed and protected.

- *Examines how sensitive data is encrypted and decrypted.*

- *Uncovers logic flaws.* The tool's discovery of an application's logic flaws is something that a web application firewall can't do.

Static-Code Analysis Limitations

There are, however, limitations to what a static-code analyzer can accomplish, including that it:

- *Requires trained software developers.* The testing involved needs to be conducted by trained software developers who fully understand the code.

- *Possibly does not support all programming languages.* A particular code analyzer might not support all programming languages.

- *Produces a false sense of security.* Static-code analysis can foster the belief that everything is being addressed, when in fact this is not always the case.

- *Is unable to find configuration problems.*

- *Cannot find runtime problems.* It cannot find vulnerabilities introduced in the runtime environment, such as authentication problems and access control issues.

- *Cannot identify insecure cryptography.*

- *Does not detect noncompliance with a security policy.*

- *Does not identify back doors.*

- *Cannot diagnose memory leaks and concurrency errors.*

- *Can be inconvenient to use.*

  Three specific ways are:

  - Automated tools can produce spurious warning/error messages that the developers cannot silence. If developers feel comfortable ignoring compiler warnings, the compile phase will eventually be filled with warnings that are ignored, even though they may include unresolved security vulnerabilities.

  - Since these tools take a long time to run, developers sometimes do not bother running them.

  - Many of these tools have difficulty analyzing code that can't be compiled. Analysts frequently can't compile code because they don't have the right libraries, all the compilation instructions, or all the code.

Dynamic-Code Analysis Advantages

Dynamic-code analysis has several advantages, particularly in identifying runtime security flaws. It can:

- *Identify vulnerabilities in a runtime environment.* Dynamic-code analysis deals with real runtime values, which static-code analysis cannot do.

- *Test applications when there is no access to the actual code.*

- *Find false negatives.* This analysis can identify vulnerabilities that might have been false negatives in the static-code analysis.

- *Provide validation of static-code analysis findings.*

- *Detect vulnerabilities that static analysis cannot.*

Dynamic-Code Analysis Limitations

Dynamic-code testing technology is not perfect and does exhibit some limitations. In particular, it has limited scope. A dynamic-code tester will test for all activities it is directed to test, but if certain options or activities are not specified to the tool, it may miss testing those options or activities.

Multilayered Defense

The ideal approach is to perform both an application code review and a vulnerability test, as completing both provides the best multilayered defense.

There is a wide variety of testing tools, within both commercially available and open-source tools. These tools may be found by doing a search for static or dynamic-code analysis testing tools as well as referencing both the OWSAP and the NIST web sites.

Security Technology for Protecting Web Applications and Their Environments

A highly popular technology for protecting web applications is the web application firewall (WAF). In my opinion, the WAF is an effective countermeasure for insufficient security within a web application but it is not a replacement for sufficient security within a web application. The WAF is a countermeasure that acts as a proxy or middleman to filter data entering and leaving a web application and, in theory, to restrict the passage of malicious data. The WAF:

- *Is analogous to a network firewall.* The WAF performs an analogous role to the more widely known network firewall. The WAF is also a traffic-filtering device that sits between the web application to be protected and the Internet.

- *Filters traffic for known application vulnerabilities.* In doing so, the WAF will drop potentially threatening inbound or outbound traffic. Its filter rules need to be continuously updated with the latest vulnerabilities in order to optimize the effectiveness of the technology.

There are, of course, many other relevant application security technologies that help provide defense in depth, including antivirus, antispam, antimalware, web application and network vulnerability scanners, authentication mechanisms, strong authentication mechanisms, intrusion detection systems, intrusion preventions systems, and the list goes on.

It is my opinion that WAFs should be considered as a piece of a well-thought-out complete security environment but should not replace developing secure application environments and testing them accordingly.

Summary

Web application vulnerabilities can often be prevented simply by incorporating IT security into the development process right up front. A valuable process is to build security right into the software development life cycle, which includes rules and guidance on how to securely write code. Testing code using either or both static-code and dynamic-code testing technology during the coding process provides massive downstream benefits in terms of eliminating vulnerabilities that would have to otherwise be found and remediated at future times. WAFs are an excellent adjunct to, but not a replacement for, a secure code development and testing process.

In summary:

- Prevention trumps remediation.

- Effective prevention of vulnerabilities starts with implementing security—in the software development life cycle, or SDLC.

- Financial factors should be considered when deciding whether to include strong security practices within the SDLC.

- There exist strong frameworks for writing secure application code, called security-in-software development life cycles, or S-SDLC.

- Incorporating security into the code-writing process is critically important.

- Web application security testing is a must during development, and it is important to make sure it is ongoing in production mode. Test. Test. Test.

- A plethora of security technologies exist for protecting web applications and their environment.

- Web application firewalls are an excellent security technology but should not replace secure coding practices and vulnerability testing. WAFs are best used as part of a defense in depth.

■ ■ ■

CHAPTER 6

How to Manage Security on Applications Written by Third Parties

Many web site owners use third-party software for their web applications and the underlying web application environment. The actual web applications may be off the shelf or developed by a third party on behalf of a web site owner. The web server, the server operating system, and the back-end database are a few common examples.

All the liability that may result from security breaches on web applications is the responsibility of site owners even though all the control for the security posture of all the third-party vendor code is with the third-party software vendors. Therefore, the site owners need to ensure that they maximize their legal leverage over their third-party software vendors in order to provide all security features and timely upgrades/patches in a timely fashion.

Maximizing site owners' legal leverage is the subject of this chapter. Since the author is not a lawyer, when translating these recommendations into a contract, you will require legal assistance, preferably from a lawyer with substantial experience in software-support contract law.

Transparency of Problem Resolution

Transparency of problem resolution is the key to managing third parties. This applies equally to the security of applications written by third parties. Problems arise when site owners identify security issues and request fixes in the form of upgrades or patches from their third-party vendors. These problems include:

- vendors not acknowledging the problems

- vendors being overly slow to acknowledge the problems

- vendors acknowledging the problems but not agreeing to fix them

- vendors agreeing to fix the problems but not committing to a timeline

- vendors committing to a timeline but missing the milestones and the deadline

- the upgrade or patch being delivered but failing to fix the problem

- the upgrade or patch fixing the problem but causing other problems

In cases of software that is widely used and produced by large companies such as Microsoft or Oracle, the site owner will not have much say in a support contract. In cases where the application is not widely sold or where the software is uniquely written or tuned for a site owner, the site owner has more leverage to ask for a stringent support agreement.

What follows are some specific recommendations for the site owner with leverage over the software vendor to ensure that the site owner and software vendor have a clear view of the other's needs and expectations.

It is up to site owners to ensure that they have a written support contract in place with their third-party software vendor and that the agreement contains all of their requirements. The support contract must be read and approved by the site owner's lawyers prior to signing.

The contract should state that:

- There is a written service-level agreement (SLA) for managing problem resolution that includes specific mechanisms for the site owners to issue a request/problem resolution and for the vendor to respond, response time frames for communications, and response time for problem resolution.

- There are written remedies and time to remediate compliance violations if either party fails to comply.

- It includes a patch/upgrade schedule and provides an accompanying description of the exact responsibilities of the third-party software vendor to provide and implement patches/upgrades, including a rollback process in the case of failed patches /upgrades.

- Source code will be kept in escrow by a third-party escrow agent and will be made available to the site owner in the instance where the third-party software vendor can no longer adhere to the support contract. It should also state that source code will be made available irrespective of any legal complexities relating to change of ownership or the financial viability of the vendor.

- It has an explicit escalation path for any issue that is not being resolved in accordance with the steps and timing described in the support contract. The escalation path should contain the titles, names, office/cell/home phone numbers, e-mail addresses, and business addresses of all personnel in both the site owner's organization and the third-party software vendor's organization.

- The third-party software vendor will either hire outside security experts—a fourth party in this case—to conduct regular vulnerability assessments of the application and compose an assessment report that it will make available to the site owner, or agree to allow the site owner to conduct regular vulnerability assessments on the application.

It should additionally state that the costs of the regular vulnerability assessments will be borne by the third-party software vendor and, just as important, that the costs of remediating any discovered vulnerabilities will be borne by the vendor.

Liability Insurance as Backup for Transparency of Problem Resolution

Since a site owner's liability does not necessarily transfer to a third-party software developer in the case of a security breach caused by a failure in a software support agreement, I advise a couple of ways of managing the liability for a security breach: either with insurance or with a written guarantee from the software vendor to take responsibility for the costs associated with a security breach. Costs may be both direct and indirect consequential damages to other parties.

However, even if the third-party software vendor undertakes responsibility for the costs of a security breach, it is strongly advisable to ensure it has liability insurance in force at all times to cover the liability contingency.

Change Management

Change management for third-party applications should follow standard software development life cycle (SDLC) procedures, including:

- running all changes/upgrades/patched software in a test environment

- obtaining written sign-off from all user groups and from the security department for all changes

- maintaining a software library of executable code of the application, including revision numbers, patch numbers, and change dates

It is widely understood that contracting parties will often struggle through a failing process and maintain the illusion of a successful work in progress rather than admit defeat and start over.

But starting over trumps failure.

Summary

It is important to maintain transparency in the problem-solving process, specifically because it is a web site owner's responsibility to manage any liability that is the result of a security breach occurring on his web site. This is true even if the security breach occurs on software provided by a third-party software vendor. In this case, liability does not automatically shift from a web site owner to a third-party software vendor.

Wherever possible, a web application site owner should get a software support contract with transparency of problem resolution. The site owner should have her lawyer vet the agreement prior to signing. The contract should state precisely how and when support will be provided along with giving an enforceable escalation plan. Liability insurance should be considered as a backup plan to the software service contract.

It is also important that change management for third-party applications follows standard SDLC procedures. It is required the applications' adherence to these procedures is transparent.

■ ■ ■

CHAPTER 7

Integrating Compliance with Web Application Security

Compliance with regulations and industry standards is a strong motivator in today's IT security world. Regulatory standards deal mostly with financial reporting, privacy, and IT security for the protection of critical assets. Industry standards for corporate IT security are created as trusted benchmarks that corporate executives can rely upon as reasonable goals. Guidelines are less formal and just suggestions.

Compliance specifically means following the rules or control points within the applicable regulation or standard. It often falls into the security domain and therefore into the web application world simply because security vulnerabilities are also compliance violations.

The most common compliance requirements come from government regulations, industry standards, and recommendations from the outside financial auditors of publicly traded companies. Government regulations and industry standards are subject to change and publiushed publicly.

Regulations, Standards, and Expert Organization Recommendations

This section identifies some of the most widely adopted regulations and standards, as well as expert information sources. The reason why the expert recommendations are of such great value is that they are more granular and reflect current risks, while regulations and standards define requirements at a higher level. One could regard regulations and standards as operating at the strategic level, while the expert organizations provide tactical recommendations.

The regulations discussed in this book span all aspects of security and cover various geographic and industry types by jurisdiction. It should be noted there are many more regulations than mentioned here and no doubt many more will come into existence.

Government Regulations

Some of the more well-known governmental regulations that require IT security compliance to various degrees are:

- **California Security Breach Information Act (SB-1386)**: privacy

- **Health Insurance Portability and Accountability Act (HIPAA)**: privacy of medical records

- **Ontario Securities Commission (OSC) Bill 198**: financial reporting

- **North American Electric Reliability Corporation Critical Infrastructure Protection 02 -09 (NERC CIP 02-09)**: electrical utility security

- **Personal Information Protection and Electronic Documents Act (PIPEDA)**: privacy

- **Harmonized Threat and Risk Assessment Methodology by the Chief, Communications Security Establishment and the Royal Canadian Mounted Police / RCMP/CSE TRA**: security

- **Sarbanes-Oxley Act (SOX)**: financial reporting

Industry Standards

The following is a good representation of security and privacy regulations:

- *Control Objectives for Information and Related Technology 5 for IT Security* (COBIT 5 for IT Security): This is a security standard that provides guidance to help IT and security professionals understand, utilize, implement, and direct important information about security-related activities.

- *Experian Independent Third Party Assessment* (E13PA): Addressing both security and privacy, this document identifies certification requirements for third parties that want direct electronic access to Experian credit-history information.

- *Global Data Synchronization for GS1 Data Pools* (GS1): This is a security guideline for all members of the GS1, which is a nonprofit organization that creates guidelines for companies that exchange information electronically. The GS1 is well known for producing barcode standards.

- *International Standards Organization 27002 and 17799* (ISO 27002 and ISO 17799): The ISO 27002 is an information security standard that was published in 2002 and gives recommendations for IT security controls, which are actions or technology used to reduce the chance of a security breach. It has since been republished as ISO 17799.

- *PCI Data Security Standard* (PCI DSS): Created by the PCI Security Standards Council, this standard covers security and privacy guidelines for the credit card industry.

- *Health Insurance Portability and Accountability Act* (HIPAA): This privacy regulation, presided over by the US Department of Health and Human Services, protects the privacy of individuals' health information.

Recommendations from Expert Organizations

There is a wealth of open-source web application security assistance found in expert organization publications. This information can serve as both an adjunct to and assistance for adherence to control points required by regulations and industry standards. Some of the organizations that produce recommendations are:

- **International Information Systems Security Certification Consortium** (ISC2): Focusing on both security and privacy, this organization is the designator of the Certified Information Security System Professional (CISSP) and other security certifications.

- **Information Systems Audit and Control Association**: ISACA is the creator of COBIT 5 and COBIT 5 for IT Security and the designator of Certified Information Security Manager (CISM) and other security certifications.

- **National Institute of Standards and Technology**: NIST is the federal technology agency that works with industry to develop and apply technology, measurements, and standards.

- **Open Web Application Security Project**: OWASP is a worldwide not-for-profit organization focused on improving web application security and providing information that helps make informed decisions about true software security risks.

- **SANS**: This information-security training organization derived its name from the first letters of SysAdmin, Audit, Networking, and Security. SANS both provides training and publishes the *Critical Security Controls Version 5 List*, which is a regularly updated list of what SANS considers to be the most serious IT security vulnerabilities for the reporting period.

- **Web Application Security Consortium**: WASC is an international group of experts, industry practitioners, and organizational representatives who produce open-source and widely agreed-upon best-practice security standards for the World Wide Web.

Financial Auditors' Favorites

The following guidelines are the compliance requirements recommended by financial auditors for both IT security and work flow control point compliance. I have included these guidelines in this section because they are widely referenced by third-party financial auditors as being their clients' definitive guides for IT security posture, but in reality, none of these auditors have anything to do with IT security or with web application security.

- *Canadian Institute of Chartered Accountants CICA 5970*: Now superseded by the CASE 3416, CICA 5970 is a new Canadian auditing standard that is closely aligned with the US SSAE 16 and international ISAE 3402 auditing standards for evaluating internal controls for financial auditing.

- *COBIT 5*: As previously discussed, COBIT 5 is ISACA's business framework for the governance and management of enterprise IT.

- *ITIL*: Formerly known as the IT Infrastructure Library, ITIL is the most widely accepted standard in the world for how to plan, deliver, and support IT service features.

- *American Institute of Certified Public Accountants' Statement of Auditing Standards No. 70 for Service Organizations* (SAS 70): SAS 70 is the examination standard for auditors and often includes controls for information technology and related processes.

Leading Standards and Regulations

I believe that the PCI DSS, the E13PA, the NERC CIP, and COBIT 5 are the frontrunners for IT security standards, with some overlap on web application security. These regulations and industry standards along with SOX, the ISO 27000, and the NIST 800-53 are described in a little more detail in this section. The most relevant sections of the standards are included in the appendices of this book, as referred to in Table 7-1. They are included here with the kind written permission of the source organizations.

Table 7-1. *Standards Covered in the Appendices in This Book*

Appendix	Standard	Subject matter
Appendix A	COBIT 5 for IT Security	Best security practices; widely used by IT Security auditors
Appendix B	E13PA	Version of the PCI DSS adapted by Experian
Appendix C	ISO 27000	A high-level framework for IT security
Appendix D	NERC CIP	Critical infrastructure protection for electrical, water, and sewage utilities with sections pertinent to web application security
Appendix E	NIST 800-53	US government IT security recommendations
Appendix F	PCI DSS	Security for credit card vendors, with many useful sections for web application security
Appendix G	Sarbanes-Oxley (SOX)	Accuracy requirements for financial reporting, but lacks specific security recommendations

The following sections provide an overview of each standard, offering convenient reference points to which to refer when you look at the actual appendices.

COBIT

COBIT is really a short-form name for the most recent version of a constantly evolving standard that provides a business framework for the governance and management of enterprise IT. The most current version is COBIT 5. It is a favorite of external financial auditors, especially for setting IT security control points for their clients. There is also a version of COBIT specifically for information security, which I will discuss in the next section.

ISACA is the author of both COBIT, the business framework, and COBIT 5 for IT Security, in addition to other standards. ISACA, previously known as the Information Systems Audit and Control Association, is an independent nonprofit global association. It engages in the development, adoption, and use of globally accepted, industry-leading knowledge and practices for information systems.

The SOX standard, which is derived from the Sarbanes-Oxley Act and is covered later in this chapter, relies on COBIT and dovetails well with the responsibilities of financial auditors. Since COBIT is highly methodical and process oriented, it is relatively easy for financial auditors to translate it into measurable control points. As previously mentioned, security controls or control points are actions or technology used to reduce the chance of a security breach. Controls can be used to reduce exposure to threats, to reduce occurrence of vulnerabilities, and to reduce the chance of a vulnerability being compromised by a threat.

■ **Note**   An excellent list of security controls, *Critical Security Controls*, Version 5, is published by SANS.

COBIT 5 for IT Security

COBIT 5 for IT Security is a different publication than COBIT, previously mentioned. As its name indicates, COBIT 5 for IT Security is more on topic for security matters. The similar names can be confusing, and even some security people are not aware that there are two different standards published by ISACA.

E13PA and PCI DSS

Both the E13PA, produced by Experian, and the PCI DSS, produced by the PCI Security Standards Council, are excellent granular standards for financial transaction web sites and their associated network infrastructures. The E13PA is an auditing standard that is based on the PCI DSS standard. These standards are more architecturally and implementation oriented than COBIT, but, of course, all three standards deal with policies and procedures.

The PCI DSS, or *PCI Data Security Standard*, is a framework for developing a robust payment card data security process, which includes prevention, detection, and appropriate reaction to security incidents. The PCI Security Standards Council is an open global forum launched in 2006 that is responsible for the development, management, education, and awareness of the PCI Security Standards. The council's five founding global payment brands are American Express, Discover Financial Services, JCB International, MasterCard, and Visa.

Experian is an information services company that helps businesses to manage credit risk, prevent fraud, target marketing offers, and automate decision making. The company also helps individuals to check their credit report and credit score and protect against identity theft. The E13PA, or *Experian Independent 3rd Party Assessment*, is a comprehensive list of the IT security control points that comprise Experian's security requirements for a business partner, such as a reseller of Experian data that communicates with the Experian network. Although EI3PA is licensed by PCI, it focuses on protecting Experian data.

ISO 27000

Ubiquitously held in high esteem, the ISO 27000 series is the basis for creating both security architectural frameworks and IT security audits.

The International Organization for Standards (ISO) develops and publishes internal standards with the goal of ensuring the safety, reliability, and quality of products and services. One of its standards is the ISO 27001 for Information Security and Management.

NIST

NIST, the American National Institute for Standards and Technology, publishes an array of recommendations for all matters related to IT, including the most recent NIST 800-53, which deals with IT Security.

NIST is the US federal technology agency that works with industry to develop and apply technology, measurements, and standards, including those for IT security.

NERC CIP

The *North American Electric Reliability Corporation's Critical Infrastructure Protection standard*, or NERC CIP, is one of my favorites, as it is both architecturally detailed and constantly evolving. Technical detail is seen in Appendix D, which contains the relevant sections of CIP-007-5, where some detailed control point references for application security are given. Appendix D also addresses updating, giving relevant subsets of tables identifying current enforcements and those areas subject to future enforcement. The future enforcement sections contain augmentations to existing control points and new control points.

The expert organizations' documentation have far more detail and depth of recommendations than NERC CIP, as do the E13PA and the PCI DSS, and NERC CIP does not focus on web application security to the extent that the publications of these other organizations do.

The NERC CIP was created as a direct response to the Department of Homeland Security's requirement for a secure, reliable electricity infrastructure for the United States. As such, the standard focuses around the primary application used by electrical utilities called SCADA. However, the NERC CIP can be applied to almost any IT security architecture.

Sarbanes-Oxley

The Sarbanes-Oxley Act, or SOX, does not really have any prescriptive directions for IT security, as its primary focus is on the accuracy of financial reporting. As such, SOX primarily relies upon COBIT for an IT security framework. The specific COBIT document for this purpose is called *IT Control Objectives for Sarbanes-Oxley*, 2nd Edition. The SOX bill does not refer to ISACA or COBIT in any way; however, COBIT has become the de facto standard for SOX compliance.

Integrating Compliance and Security Reporting

I described vulnerability reporting in Chapter 3 and remediation reporting in Chapter 4. I also identified compliance regulations, standards, and guidelines earlier in this chapter. It now is time to put all the aspects together in a clear, understandable way.

Since compliance with a security standard involves identifying any underlying security vulnerability that may cause a compliance violation, it is very simple to combine compliance with a security audit. Any security vulnerability found during an audit that impinges upon a compliance standard is simply noted as a compliance violation. If you will, this is hitting two birds with one stone.

The most expedient way to accomplish combining reporting on compliance with web application security is to simply incorporate both within one reporting table. If compliance to any standard or standards is part of a security policy, it is useful to cross-reference the relevant subsections of applicable documents in the technical sections of corporate security policy/procedures documents and of course within the results of web-application-security vulnerability assessments.

An easy way to accomplish creating this table of integrated vulnerabilities, remediation, and compliance is to build on an existing table. Included with the downloads for this book is a summary table of vulnerabilities, remediation for each vulnerability, and its associated risk. A logical approach to adding compliance is simply to create a new column heading across the top of the table for each compliance requirement. A compliance requirement may be a regulatory requirement such as SOX, an industry compliance requirement such as COBIT 5, or a requirement to comply with corporate IT security policy. If the requirement were to involve complying with COBIT 5, PCI, and corporate policy, then the table headings would be as shown in Table 7-2. These three compliance requirements would make sense together in a case like this:

- The corporate external financial auditor specifies several COBIT control points as requirements to pass an annual audit.

- Retail credit card payments are a key process of the corporation's day-to-day business activities, and the corporation must adhere to the PCI DSS.

In Table 7-2, three compliance columns have been added to correlate the vulnerabilities with the compliance violations of COBIT 5 for IT Security, the PCI DSS, and corporate security policy standards.

Table 7-2. Summary of Risk and Remediation, with Compliance Standards Added

Vulnerability class	Risk	Description	Remediation summary	COBIT 5 for IT Security violation	PCI DSS violation	Corporate policy violation
Lack of Sufficient Authentication	High	Prior to accessing a web application, a server should require end users to authenticate themselves and confirm they are in fact who they purport to be.	*Create password strength.* Passwords should be required to have a minimum size and complexity. Complexity typically requires the use of minimum combinations of alphabetic, numeric, and/or nonalphanumeric characters in a user's password (e.g., at least one of each).	Figure 55: User Access and Access Rights Services	4.1.e: Secure Configurations	Authentication: password strength and password renewal schedule
Weak session management	High	Session management is something that most users are unaware of. It is an essential security methodology for foiling hackers from attempting to break into and take control of a session. The idea is for a server to be able to regularly verify that the user interaction or conversation is the one the server thinks it is.	*Encrypt all transactions.* Encrypt all transactions between web browsers and web applications with the SSL or TLS protocol so that your application runs on an SSL/HTTPS-secured site.	Figure 58: Protection Against Malware and Attack Services	4.1.1: Weak Encryption	Encryption of client/servers sessions: requirement for most updated SSL version

Weak access control	High	Restricting or controlling access to an application, or for that matter to all important processes and files, is the most important aspect of security. Conversely, a prime goal of hackers is to gain unauthorized access and then increase the priority level of their access privileges.	*Restrict unauthorized access to applications and servers.* Ensure that unauthorized users cannot gain access to functions to which they should not have access at the application and server levels.	Figure 56: User access and access rights goals	4.1.e: Secure Configurations	Access control: enforcement for user authorization occurring on the application and validated at the server
Weak input validation at the application level	High	Unauthorized access is the golden nugget for hackers. A strong protection against unauthorized access is sufficient validation of the identities of users requesting access to an application.	Since access control is paramount security, strong validation is required within a web application both for authentication and validation of input.	Figure 58: Protection Against Malware and Attack Services	4.1.e: Secure Configurations	Same as for "Access Control"

The description and remediation summaries have been abbreviated in this example. See Chapters 3 and 4, or the summary table in the downloads for this book, for the complete descriptions. The references within the standards columns are to figures and sections in those standards.

Summary

Compliance is a strong motivator to enforce rigorous IT security and web application security. Most compliance requirements are acted upon in order to adhere to government regulations and security control points specified by corporate external financial auditors. Sometimes, corporate policy that addresses web application security also requires adherence.

The most commonly specified regulations/standards for security-related compliance are COBIT, COBIT 5 for IT Security, the E13PA, the ISO 27000, the NERC CIP, NIST, the PCI DSS, and Sarbanes-Oxley. All of these regulations and standards have their differences.

Security-compliance control points will also always be security control points. The remediation is the same for both.

A straightforward way of reporting both security vulnerabilities and compliance violations is by using a table showing the correlation of security vulnerabilities with compliance violations. Several security regulations and standards can be referenced in one table along with security vulnerabilities.

■ ■ ■

CHAPTER 8

How to Create a Business Case for Web Application Security

The security of web applications, particularly those that are transaction platforms and those in a constant state of change, is costly to achieve and to maintain. Now, pile on privacy and regulatory-compliance testing and remediating, and the related costs become frustrating to senior managers who see no tangible or visible improvement to the web applications. These expenses must be cost justified in terms of risk and return on investment.

The key to getting the IT security governance committee to fund the appropriate compliance budget is to speak its language. In order to do that, risks need to be expressed in terms of the costs for executives. Specifically, expenses need to be identified as: potential cost of losses, mitigation costs, the total costs (potential cost of losses plus mitigation costs), and residual costs.

In order to be clear and meaningful for the intended audience, the material should be presented graphically, with changes depicted in both cost and risk over time. This trending analysis will be the most useful in supporting the IT security governance committee's ability to make well-informed decisions about how to most effectively invest in security and thereby derive optimal payback for stakeholders.

The steps to performing this analysis are:

1. Assess the risk.

2. Calculate the annual loss expectancy.

3. Calculate the cost of prevention and remediation.

4. Calculate the return on security investment (ROSI).

5. Create a business case.

6. Measure and cost justify residual risk.

7. Determine whether ROSI objectives are met.

Assessing the Risk

The first step in this process is to identify risk from a business perspective and then quantify the cost impact that would take place if the risk becomes a reality. For instance, you might identify the damage to the brand that would result from a Trojan attack causing the theft of clients' credit card information. The risk is assessed as the potential money lost as a result of a single incidence of the event, which might be $10 million. The annual loss expectancy is calculated by multiplying the estimated number of occurrences of this particular event; in this case, each at a cost of $10 million.

Identifying Risk and Its Business Impact

The costs of IT security risk associated with web applications for breaches and noncompliance of regulatory/standards and the resulting negative impact on business can be broadly identified as follows:

- loss of revenue or production due to unavailability of production resource

- time and effort needed to recover from a security-related loss of production

- legal ramifications and expenses

- damage to brand

- regulatory compliance violations

- privacy compliance violations

- damage to client and vendor relationships

- loss of intellectual, competitive, or proprietary information

- unrealized profits resulting from the inability to demonstrate to clients/vendors/partners a strong security process

The cost of risk is the resulting impact on business that may be incurred should a risk become a reality. Determining the cost of a potential event is difficult at best. However, it can be accomplished by employing one or more quantitative and qualitative methods, and should be undertaken by those most qualified to do so. Qualified assessors include unit profit and loss managers, stakeholders, and executives with insight into how an event would quantitatively affect their work domain.

The cost of various types of events can be viewed in terms of being low, medium, or high. This qualitative analysis is not useful in itself but may assist management in determining how to prioritize the order in which it will perform a more in-depth risk analysis.

Estimating the Chance of Occurrence of Each Event

Creating a case to present to senior management about web application security involves calculating the estimated cost of risk versus the cost of preventing or remediating its causes. In order to calculate the cost of risk, it is first necessary to estimate the chance of each security event occurring over the course of a budget year. To do this, you would first identify the types of threats, then use either qualitative or quantitative risk analysis, and finally calculate annual loss expectancy by associating a cost with each security event.

Once you determine the likelihood of an event occurring over the course of a budget year, the most useful way of expressing that likelihood is as a percentage representing the possibility of the event or total number of events occurring in any one year.

However, any likelihood estimate should be adjusted to account for changes in the security environment. There are typically evolving waves of new threats that may affect the likelihood of occurrence, such as:

- new Internet-based security attacks

- new viruses

- malware of all sorts

- distributed denial of service attacks (DDOS)

- identity theft

- risk created internally within the host organization of a web application, simply through the process of change and maintenance of the application and its environment

Qualitative and Quantitative Risk Analysis

As part of risk analysis, one needs to determine the chance of an event occurring. There are two basic approaches to determining the probability of an event occurring. They are: qualitative, which is more subjective and based upon commonsense and current knowledge about security issues, and quantitative, which relies upon published statistical information about chances of occurrences and mathematical calculations.

The qualitative method is the one most often used, as it is intuitively understood and most quick to estimate. It is done by first considering various events in terms of their risk and the relative cost of loss per occurrence. Then, you plot out where each vulnerability would fall in terms of threat and vulnerability levels using a graph like the one in Figure 8-1.

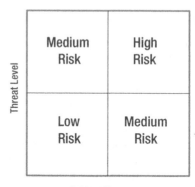

Figure 8-1. *Potential cost versus probability of occurrence*

In Figure 8-1, the cost of loss is plotted along the vertical axis and the percentage of the probability of occurrence is plotted along the horizontal axis. For any vulnerability, the higher the chance of occurrence and the higher the cost, the higher its risk. The highest risks reside in the upper-right-hand quadrant and the lowest risks, in the lower-left-hand quadrant.

Quantitative analysis is more theoretical and based upon the statistical probability of any type of event occurring in an environment. The probability is derived from the historical trends for that particular industry and geography, and should include other relevant statistical factors. I mention it here only for completeness, but it is not very practical.

Calculating Annual Loss Expectancy

The annual loss expectancy (ALE) is the estimated annualized cost for the occurrence of any type of event. This number is useful for comparison with the annual cost of mitigation. The ALE for an event is calculated by multiplying the estimated cost of a single event by the number of times it is expected to occur. The calculation is done as follows:

$$ALE = \text{estimated cost per event} \times \text{the number of estimated occurrences per year}$$

For example, if the estimated cost per a particular event is $100,000, and the estimated number of occurrences per year is 2, then:

$$ALE = \$100,000 \times 2$$

and the annual loss expectancy is $200,000.

The annual loss expectancy combined with the qualitative risk level provides decision criteria for prioritizing the order in which risks are dealt with. You can feed all this information directly into the business case covered later in this chapter in the section "Creating the Business Case for Executives." The cost of required mitigation or remediation is considered when prioritizing a risk management plan and is discussed in the next section, "Calculating the Cost of Prevention and Remediation."

Various methods can be used either separately or together with the implementation of an averaging metric to estimate the cost per occurrence of an event. These methods may include:

- soliciting expert advice from financial management, lawyers, and risk management consultants

- conducting a straw poll of stakeholders, each estimating the downside cost of an event

- participating in a fact-gathering survey of similar businesses, each of which provides factual and straw poll estimates of the cost of an event

- purchasing statistical information from industry experts regarding the cost of an event

- obtaining statistical information from industry associations about the cost of an event experienced by their membership

Calculating the Cost of Prevention and Remediation

The security team needs to identify all preventative countermeasures and remediation steps that will be taken, at least as a first-pass estimate, in order to include these items in the cost-justification business case that will be made to executives.

These steps should include hiring personnel to assist in creating policy and in executing it via implementing procedures and processes. They must also include creating control points and recommending technology and security services. The technology may be purchased, leased, or outsourced. The services similarly may be built in house, such as in-house web application auditing, or a less biased way is to outsource that service.

Once all the costs are known or estimated, they can be combined with the estimated cost of risk to come up with return-on-security investment calculations, as shown in the next section.

Calculating the Return on Security Investment

Once the total cost of security mitigation is determined, factoring in any costs for managing residual risk, calculating the ROSI, becomes straightforward. It is done as follows:

$$ROSI = cost\ of\ mitigation \div cost\ of\ risk$$

For example, if the estimated cost of mitigation is $20,000, and the estimated cost of risk is $200,000:

$$ROSI = \$20,000 \div \$200,000$$

and ROSI is 10%.

When calculating ROSI, it is important to allocate mitigation costs on a prorated basis across all risks to which they apply. This allows profit-and-loss managers and associated stakeholders to most accurately calculate and evaluate ROSI.

Executives comprehend the value of web application security with more clarity when the variables are expressed in terms of dollars and relative risk. It is more likely an executive committee will respond to a security budget if they can understand:

- the potential cost of losses associated with a security breach

- the relative risk of a breach(es) occurring within a specific period of time, such as within the next budget year

- the cost of reducing the relative risk

- the amount by which the relative risk is reduced based on the investment-in-security expenditures

A powerful method of estimating the damage of a web-application-security breach is to list the most likely outcomes of a breach and ask the members of the executive committee to ballpark the resulting costs in an executive straw poll. For instance, the outcomes may be:

- loss of production for one day

- loss of production for one week

- loss of electronic communications with clients for two days

- incorrect information collected and presented on the client support web site

The estimated annualized cost due to security breaches needs to incorporate several factors:

- the estimated cost of each breach

- the potential number of breaches during a one-year period

- the risk of a breach or breaches actually occurring
- the tolerance of the governance committee to sustaining such a breach. This is an emotional factor, which, in the author's experience, simply cannot be ignored.

The ability to estimate the potential number of breaches in a year is very difficult to estimate since it is based on many complex, difficult-to-research factors, including:

- statistical estimated similar breaches for similar industries
- estimates of new Internet threats

For expediency, it is useful to combine the estimated cost of each breach and the guesstimated number of breaches into a single number at the time of completing the straw poll. So, we may include as breaches a virus infection and a web site compromise that lead to theft of client financial information.

Three spreadsheets compiled based on a straw poll are shown in Tables 8-1 through 8-3. For clarity, separate tables are devoted to cost, risk, and tolerance. The tables illustrate three of the seven event descriptions from the section "Identifying Risk and Its Business Impact." The additional spreadsheets are included with the downloads for this book.

Table 8-1. *Cost Estimates for Various Web Application Security Events Based on Straw Poll*

Employee	Revenue loss from damaged client relationships	Revenue loss due to the inability to process transactions	Damage to brand or corporate image due to inability to process transactions	...	Impact to corporate annual revenues
CIO	$1,000,000	$100,000	$150,000		$165,000,000
CFO	$1,100,000	$150,000	$250,000		$165,000,000
CEO	$1,500,000	$20,000	$300,000		$165,000,000
Board member	$300,000	$200,000	$400,000		$165,000,000
VP of Sales	$400,000	$500,000	$175,000		$165,000,000
Average	**$860,000**	**$194,000**	**$255,000**	**...**	**$165,000,000**

In Table 8-2, the assessment of risk varies from .0 to 1, where 0 represents zero risk and 1 represents maximum risk. The numbers represented as fractions between 0 and 1 in the table indicate each manager's assessment of risk for each event.

Table 8-2. *Adjustment for Risk for Various Web Application Security Events Based on Straw Poll*

Employee	Revenue loss from damaged client relationships	Revenue loss due to the inability to process transactions	Damage to brand or corporate image due to inability to process transactions
CIO	0.4	0.6	0.3
CFO	0.3	0.5	0.2
CEO	0.2	0.4	0.1
Board member	0.5	0.7	0.4
VP of Sales	0.4	0.6	0.3
Average	**0.36**	**0.56**	**0.26**

In Table 8-3, the tolerance for risk varies from .0 to 1, where 0 represents maximum tolerance to risk and 1 represents minimum tolerance to risk. The numbers represented as fractions between 0 and 1 in the chart indicate each manager's tolerance for risk for each event. It should be noted that indicating a zero essentially means the manager will accept the risk, no matter the potential financial cost of a resulting security breach.

Table 8-3. *Adjustment for Tolerance for Various Web Application Security Events Based on Straw Poll*

Employee	Revenue losses from damaged client relationships	Revenue loss due to the inability to process transactions	Damage to brand or corporate image due to inability to process transactions
CIO	1.0	0.6	1.0
CFO	1.0	0.5	0.8
CEO	1.0	0.4	0.9
Board Member	1.0	0.7	1.0
VP Sales	1.0	0.6	0.9
Average	**1.00**	**0.56**	**0.92**

For example, from Table 8-1, the revenue loss from damaged client relationships is averaged at $860,000. From Table 8-2, the associated average risk is 0.36. Similarly, from Table 8-3, the associated tolerance for risk is 1.0. We can now represent the executives' opinion of the associated financial value of the risk along with their perceptions that the risk will actually come to fruition, along with their tolerance for the risk coming to fruition, by multiplying the three values together.

In this example, the adjusted revenue loss is expressed as

$$Adjusted\,Revenue\,Loss = Revenue\,loss \times risk \times tolerance\,for\,risk$$

or,

$$\$309,600 = \$860,000 \times 0.36 \times 1$$

Creating the Business Case for Executives

You can create a business case that justifies expenditures for web application security fairly easily created by correlating three factors:

- the cost of risk, taking into account relative risk and tolerance for risk

- the cost for preventative and remedial measures

- a variety of return-on-investment calculations

The results of the straw poll are used to create an example business case, as shown in Table 8-4. The cost of risk is detailed in Section 1, "Cost of Risk," where the cost is linked directly to the results of the straw polls and a high, medium, or low risk is assigned for each factor. For simplicity and clarity the estimates of risk and tolerance for risk are shown both as quantitative and as qualitative values in Table 8-4, which is the sample business case.

Table 8-4. *Sample Business Case for Calculating Annualized Return on Web Application Security Investment*

Section 1. Cost of Risk

Cost and/or Potential Losses from a Breach	Cost and/or Lost Revenues (Average of Respondents)	Tolerance Factor	Risk Factor	Adjustment for Risk	Adjustment for Tolerance	Adjusted Total
Revenue losses from damaged client relationships	$860,000	**Low**	**High**	0.36	1.00	$309,600
Revenue loss due to the inability to process transactions	$194,000	**Med**	**Med**	0.56	0.56	$60,838
Damage to brand or corporate image due to inability to process transactions	$255,000	**Low**	**High**	0.26	0.92	$60,996
Legal costs from client data or other third-party data made public	$70,000	**Med**	**High**	0.76	1.00	$53,200
Costs of disclosure of confidential or sensitive information which contravenes financial and disclosure regulations	$51,000	**Med**	**Med**	0.46	0.056	$13,138
Costs due to breaches of privacy and privacy regulations	$59,000	**Med**	**Low**	0.46	0.20	$5,428

(*continued*)

Table 8-4. (*continued*)

Liability and legal costs for damage to third parties	$29,000	**Low**	**High**	0.26	1.00	$7,540
Total Cost and/or Potential Losses from a Breach	**$1,518,000**					**$519,526**

Section 2: Cost to Prevent and Mitigate Potential Losses

Prevention, Countermeasure, or Mitigation	Cost
Upgrade patch management process.	$35,000
Implement all recommendations of last vulnerability assessment.	$25,000
Purchase ongoing vulnerability assessments.	$50,000
Regularly analyze all event logs.	$50,000
Upgrade authentication process.	$50,000
Upgrade web application security policy.	$25,000
Total Annual Mitigation Costs	**$235,000**

(*continued*)

Table 8-4. (*continued*)

Section 3. Cost of Risk	
Calculations of Key Cost and Risk Ratios	ROSI
Return on Security Investment (ROSI)% of $ Mitigation / $ Potential Losses	15.48%
% of $ Mitigation / $ Adjusted Potential Losses	45.23%
Client's annual revenues	$165,000,000
% of $ Mitigation / $ Annual Revenues	0.14%
% of $ Potential Losses / $ Annual Revenues	0.92%
% of $ Adjusted Potential Losses / $ Annual Revenues	0.31%

Section 2, "Cost to Prevent and Mitigate Potential Losses," shows a budget for preventative and mitigation factors related to security, as can be composed by your web application security team.

The bottom-line ratios of return on investment, risk relative to gross income, and prevention/mitigation costs relative to gross income are shown in Section 3, "Return on Investment."

Measuring and Cost-Justifying Residual Risk

Measuring residual risk is an ongoing responsibility and it is often thankless since nobody wants to hear that risk still exists after spending considerable funds on eliminating it. One of the easiest ways of identifying residual risk is to create or purchase a monthly security health score, which should include a delta report of how your security health is changing month to month. Calculating the risk associated with residual vulnerabilities is similar to the process already described in this chapter. It is always important to understand the difference between when a vulnerability is merely dealt with and when it is effectively fixed. When cost-justifying a security budget and subsequently cost-justifying it for remedial risk, everything comes down to calculating if the ROSI is satisfactory.

Calculating Security Status and Residual Risk with a Monthly Security Health Score

A simple-to-create and simple-to-convey method of estimating residual risk involves using a monthly web-application-security health report. The report is based upon statistical results of what actually occurred in the application security environment under scrutiny.

You should get a proposal of the list of factors to be considered from your security team and have it approved by the security governance committee so that the results are meaningful to all concerned. The factors will probably change over time in accordance with changes in the business environment. Examples of factors are:

- the number of high-risk vulnerabilities found during the previous month's web application vulnerability scans

- the number of high risks remediated in one day, week, month, or more than one month

- the number of servers that don't have the latest recommended security patches applied

- the number of workstations that don't have the latest recommended security patches applied

The factors, criteria of how to calculate scores for each factor, and weighting of each factor can then be tabulated in a spreadsheet, with a perfect score being 100%. The numeric score and the details of its calculation are valuable planning information, and the security governance team will be able to easily absorb a single percent or alphabetic score.

The results can be reported numerically, such as with a percentage, and alphabetically, as *A*, *B*, *C*, or *D*. It is most useful to also record scores over time in order to see a pattern of performance.

Figure 8-2 shows an example scorecard. The score is calculated by using control points to create scoring criteria. In this example, the four major scoring criteria are: server patch management, account administration, virus/spam problems, and undiagnosed security events. A score for a particular month is allocated for each criterion and a percentage-based score out of a total perfect score is calculated. The score is multiplied by applying a weighting factor for each criteria—in this case 25% weighting for each criteria—in order to come up with a total weighted score of 81%, which in turn is assigned an alphabetical value of *A-*.

Score for September 2014		A-	81%			
Control Points for Assessing Score	Weight	Score Out of 100	Possible Perfect Score	% Score	Weighted Score	
Server Patch Management	25%				16.7%	
Timeliness of patches		60	100			
Patches missed		40	100			
Failed patches		100	100			
Total		200	300	66.7%		
Account Administration	25%				20.6%	
Expired accounts not deleted		80	100			
Non authorized accounts not deleted		90	100			
Failed login attempts on admin accounts		90	100			
Failed login attempts on user accounts		70	100			
Total		330	400	82.5%		
Virus / Spam Problems	25%				23.8%	
Serious virus events		90	100			
Serious spam events		100	100			
Total		190	200	95.0%		
Undiagnosed Security Events	25%				20.0%	
Serious security events (server and IDS) not fully investigated		80	100			
Total		80	100	80.0%		
Total Weighted Score					81.0%	

Figure 8-2. *A monthly security health scorecard*

How to Cost-Justify and Triage Vulnerabilities for Remediation

We have already looked at cost-justifying remediation and calculating residual risk. However, the calculations do not take into consideration the timing or order of remediation. Deciding on the order of remediation directly impacts risk at any point in time plus the timing of expenditures necessary to remediate.

Since information security is fundamentally concerned with both risk management and optimizing the return on investment of key assets, it makes sense to triage the vulnerabilities for remediation based upon the same principles.

If your corporate security policy sets out criteria for evaluating remediation, then it is relatively simple to create a remediation plan.

The data for creating a remediation plan type starts with identifying the residual vulnerabilities, their associated risk, the number of occurrences of each vulnerability, and the estimated time to remediate each type of vulnerability, along with the associated costs of risk. The technical vulnerability information can be obtained from a web-application-security audit.

The key asset values should be documented as part of the creation of an overall IT security policy and should be regularly reviewed thereafter, particularly in organizations involved with:

- mergers and acquisitions

- sharing of data with partnering organizations

- sharing of data with customers and vendors

- creating and updating web-enabled applications

- change in general

The remediation plan can therefore be optimized according to several parameters, such as minimizing impact, remediating the most number of vulnerabilities in a given amount of time, or mitigating the highest risk vulnerabilities.

It is good security practice for the person creating the mitigation plan to share the plan in written form with management for their buy-in.

As an ongoing practice, it is useful if possible to track vulnerabilities by type, frequency of occurrence, the time lapse between discovering a vulnerability and actually beginning remediation, and time to remediate. This information is useful in identifying the root cause of problems and for getting financial justification for more IT security resources.

Noting the Difference Between Remediating and Fixing

Remediation is often confused with getting the problem *fixed*. Too often, remediation is not successful in resolving the initial vulnerability. This is particularly true when it takes place over a period of a few days or weeks after the discovery of a vulnerability, especially in dynamic environments. This is also true when remediation steps are not documented and relayed to all sources of potential change associated with the change management process.

Remediation can be undone or compromised by operational processes and can be introduced by various parties, including consultants and subcontractors as well as in-house code writers and IT/security operations staff.

It is suggested that when remediation is not successful, one should document:

- which vulnerabilities have been affected and, more important, which key assets are at risk

- why the remediation was unsuccessful or how the remediation was reversed

- recommended next steps to either reimplement the original remediation recommendation or alternative suggestions to resolve the vulnerability

It is both important and useful to keep a log of why remediation was not successful in order to identify the root causes of problems, and subsequently modifying policies and processes helps improve the change management process. This information should then be fed into the IT-security budgeting process.

Calculating the Cost of Mitigation

Security professionals are well acquainted with determining the costs of mitigation. Senior executives sometimes think they too are familiar with these costs based on ads they have read about antivirus and firewall technology.

The danger here is that it is all too easy for those concerned to focus on technology as the primary mitigation for security and compliance.

It is well advised to address the following areas of mitigation:

1. reengineering processes, both technological and human-oriented

2. security technology

3. physical security

4. training and awareness

5. third-party auditing to verify the effectiveness of all of the above

From an IT security governance perspective, the optimal cost point for mitigation is where the total costs of risk and mitigation are lowest. This point can be graphically determined, as done in Figure 8-3.

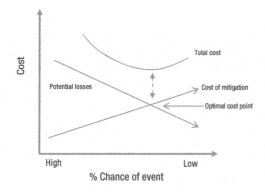

Figure 8-3. *Optimal cost point for mitigation*

Once mitigation costs are determined, it is important to express to the IT security governance committee that mitigation only goes so far and that some residual risk remains even after spending on mitigation takes place. The residual risk can be expressed as the cost of risk that remains after mitigation is implemented. As shown in Figure 8-4, expenditures on mitigation reduce the cost of exposure to risk.

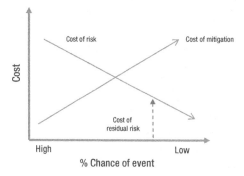

Figure 8-4. *Mitigation cost vs. % chance of event occurring*

Your IT security governance committee may decide to deal with residual risk by:

- accepting the risk

- passing on the risk (by purchasing insurance)

- further mitigation

Measuring the Effectiveness of Mitigation

It is paramount to close the risk management loop by comparing the planned and actual results of mitigation. The goal is to identify clearly whether the risk level has changed and what consistent metrics will be used to base a conclusion on. Once again, this may be difficult to accomplish directly, but there are common metrics for measuring and comparing the results of implementing mitigation. The metrics should always:

- produce repeatable, consistent results

- be understandable

- be reasonably simple to use over time

The following list of resources and frameworks provide a good initial guide to metrics that can be used for consistently measuring and reporting on risk:

- **"Incorporating Security into the Enterprise Architecture Process"**: (www.gartner.com/doc/488575/incorporating-security-enterprise-architecture-process) This white paper, offered by Gartner and produced by Enterprise Information Security Architecture (EISA), can be used as an architecture for measuring risk.

- **Architecture Framework Forum**: (www.architectureframework.com/dodaf/) This web site is devoted to enterprise architecture frameworks and technologies.

- **Institute for Enterprise Architecture Developments**: (www.enterprise-architecture.info/) The institute's web site offers the extended enterprise architecture framework (E2AF) and an information exchange area.

- **"Federal Enterprise Architecture" (FEA)**: (www.whitehouse.gov/omb/e-gov/fea/) The US Government's Office of Management and Budget offers various papers related to FEA guidance, reference models, and management tools.

- **Capgemini's integrated architecture framework**: (http://www.ca.capgemini.com/resources/the-integrated-architecture-framework-explained)

- **"NIH Enterprise Architecture Framework"**: (https://enterprisearchitecture.nih.gov/Pages/Framework.aspx) The US Government's National Institutes of Health Enterprise Architecture offers this framework outlining the enterprise information technology environment at NIH.

- **Open Security Architecture**: (www.opensecurityarchitecture.org/cms/index.php) The OSA's web site offers various information on open security architecture.

- **Open Group architecture framework**: (http://pubs.opengroup.org/architecture/togaf8-doc/arch/)

- **Zachman Framework**: (www.zachman.com/about-the-zachman-framework)

- **Control points from the COBIT framework**: (www.isaca.org/Template.cfm?Section=COBIT6&Template=/TaggedPage/TaggedPageDisplay.cfm&TPLID=55&ContentID=7981)

The following tests and trends already occurring within your company can be used to measure and report on risk:

- vulnerability assessments

- penetration tests

- time trends in frequency of occurrence and the real costs of security events, privacy violations, and policy-compliance violations

- time trends in cost to recover from events

- time trends in frequency of policy-compliance violations that do not necessarily cause any financial losses, including Trojans, viruses, root kits, unauthorized logins, attempted port scans, frequency of dropped packets, frequency of password life cycle, breaches, and frequency of rescheduled/cancelled IT security governance meetings with business managers.

Determining Whether Return on Security Investment Objectives Are Met

Tires meet the road when it is time to determine whether or not ROSI objectives for security/policy/compliance have been met. Conveying this determination is essential to building (or destroying) the credibility of the group that made the mitigation recommendations in the first place.

Determining ROSI is quite simple, as discussed previously in the "Calculating the Return on Security Investment" section. The actual costs resulting from events are compared with the projected costs after mitigation. If the mitigation was successful, then the actual costs should be near or below the projected costs. This information can be presented as shown in Figure 8-5 (an updated version of Figure 8-3). For purposes of accuracy, new trends that developed in the security environment over the period of study should be considered. If the new trends increased the cost of losses, and the effects can be quantified, then the results should be reported accordingly.

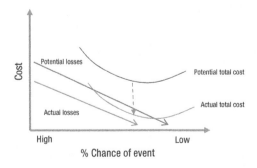

Figure 8-5. *Projected vs. actual cost of losses*

Summary

The task of getting approval for a sufficient budget for web application security, including privacy-regulatory compliance, is simplified when financial executives are presented with sufficiently clear data to build a cost-justifying business case.

The IT security governance body should request that graphic presentations of data be provided to them by the security team. The graphs should depict the relationship between the cost of risk and the cost of mitigation. The presentation process should occur both at the time of the budget request, in order to show the intended plan, and after the budget cycle, to show the actual results.

Financial managers and stakeholders should participate in a straw poll to estimate business costs resulting from potential security breaches. This is an easy way to engage them in the security process, and it will make the cost justification business case more meaningful to them. A monthly web application health scorecard is a useful tool for measuring and communicating ongoing security health and security posture for all concerned.

Residual risks and their mitigation will be ongoing and therefore will need to be included in ongoing cases made to executives for cost-justifying web application security.

CHAPTER 9

Parting Thoughts

Over the course of this book, we have covered the critical aspects of web application security. Before closing, let's look back at the salient points and steps in the web application security process.

Web application security is an ongoing process involving the executive committee, application owners, end users, the development and testing teams, and the IT security team. The process begins with analyzing the risk of application assets and the processes they affect in order to determine a starting point for assessing a security budget.

It is important to understand the differences and relationships between threats, vulnerabilities, risk, breaches, remediation, and countermeasures. These were discussed in Chapter 1.

The importance of involving the executive committee in the web application security process cannot be overstated. Reminding senior stakeholders and executives of the potential downside costs of a security breach (in a detailed assessment report) is a strong motivator for the executive committee to participate in a straw poll. The how-tos for this process were described in Chapter 8.

Gaining a more detailed understanding of vulnerabilities and their remediation is the next key step required in order to build a security program specifically for web applications. Chapters 3 and 4 covered the current threats and vulnerabilities that we find in real-life situations.

The IT group may want to acquire training and recommendations from members of organizations in the IT security establishment, which includes CERT, NIST, OWASP, ISC2, ISACA, ISO, and so forth. The IT department of any organization must reach out to third-party expertise for security audits, web application and network vulnerability assessments, penetration tests, and code reviews. It is useful for all concerned to understand the relationships between all these types of security testing. Chapter 2 provided a drill down into these topics.

While executives certainly do not need to understand the details about current threats and vulnerabilities, they do need sufficient familiarity with the concepts in order to manage their web application security team. There is a wealth of online, impartial, no-charge resources to keep executives up to date on the top trends in security issues. Organizations like OWASP, SANS, and WASC, which were mentioned in Chapter 7, provide quick reads for explaining security issues, for all levels of comprehension. As mentioned previously, a downloadable spreadsheet summarizes the top classes of vulnerabilities and their remediation identified in Chapters 3 and 4 and can be updated by the reader and kept current.

The Appendices A, B, C, D, E, F, G, and H in this book are a good resource for understanding web application security recommendations across several expert organizations. The reader will quickly see the overlap of recommendations across several of the standards and guidelines in the appendices.

The next step on the critical path of risk mitigation is to create a proposal for a web application security program that includes technology, person hours, training, end-user security awareness training, and, of course, the applicable policy and process documents. The spreadsheets in Chapter 8 are available to readers to download and modify to meet their specific planning needs. Then it's time to present management with the program budget along with estimates of risk reduction that include the benefits of reducing the potential cost of losses due to security breaches.

Once the budget is approved, it's time for the IT group and developers to swing into action and develop, deploy, mitigate, or test, as required. Chapter 5 got into some detail about building effective countermeasures for web application vulnerabilities. If third-party web application software is used, next it's time to get the software license owners involved. Chapter 6 explained the why's and how's for doing so.

If you remember anything about this book, please let it be that enforcing strong web application security policies for people, processes, and technology gives the best chances for no breaches. It is also a good prescription for sleeping more soundly at night.

APPENDIX A

■ ■ ■

COBIT® 5 for Information Security

The material in this appendix is taken from an ISACA® document titled *COBIT® 5 for Information Security*.[1] I have included it here as a convenient compliance resource to refer to since it is mentioned in Chapter 8, "Integrating Compliance with Web Application Security," and in several places throughout the book.

The information is reproduced verbatim from the ISACA publication. The references within this information include mention of Appendix B and Appendix F. For clarity, these appendices are *COBIT® 5 for Information Security* appendices and not appendices from this book. Since this is copyrighted information, I have not made any changes whatsoever.

To access the full *COBIT® 5 for Information Security* publication, please go to www.isaca.org. ISACA is an independent, nonprofit, global association that engages in the development, adoption, and use of globally accepted, industry-leading knowledge and practices for information systems. ISACA® and COBIT® are trademarks registered by ISACA® in the United States and other countries.

---

[1]Excerpt from Information Systems Audit and Control Association, "Appendix F: Detailed Guidance: Services, Infrastructure and Application Enabler," in *COBIT® 5 for Information Security* (Rolling Hills, IL: ISACA, 2012). Reprinted with the permission of ISACA®.

F.3 Secure Development
Description of the Service Capability

Figure 45 describes the service capability for secure development services.

Figure 45—Secure Development Services: Description of the Service Capability	
Service Capability	**Description**
Develop secure coding practices.	The design and delivery of coding practices, examples and content demonstrating secure coding and development (development of code that can withstand attacks) for a given set of languages and environments
Develop secure infrastructure libraries.	The design and delivery of language- and environment-specific information security modules that provide essential or critical information security functions

Attributes

Figure 46 describes attributes for secure development services.

Figure 46—Secure Development Services: Attributes		
Service Capability	**Supporting Technology**	**Benefit**
Develop secure coding practices.	• Compilers, linkers • Secure coding resources (books, courses, examples) • Static and binary analysis tools • Code scanners	• Decreased likelihood of vulnerabilities in code • Assistance in conforming with compliance standards
Develop secure infrastructure libraries.	• Development languages • Secure coding resources (books, courses) • Code scanners • Static and binary analysis tools • Compilers, linkers	• Protection of intellectual property • Decreased likelihood of vulnerabilities in software development

Goals

Figure 47 describes goals for secure development services.

Figure 47—Secure Development Services: Goals

Service Capability	Quality Goal	Metric
Develop secure coding practices.	Accurate identification of all information risk and resulting business risk/effects to a given asset or entity	Number of new types of risk discovered via incidents not covered in report
Develop secure infrastructure libraries.	Improvements in information security configuration of systems in alignment with information security requirements	Number of information security issues discovered after an information security assessment of the hardened system

F.4 Security Assessments
Description of the Service Capability

Figure 48 describes the service capability for security assessment services.

Figure 48—Security Assessment Services: Description of the Service Capability

Service Capability	Description
Perform information security assessments.	Performance of an information security assessment of a given entity, system, process, procedure, application or organisational unit for information security issues
Perform information risk assessments.	Process of providing identification, evaluation, estimation and analysis of threats to and vulnerabilities of an given entity, system, process, procedure, application or organisational unit to determine the levels of risk involved (potential for losses), and using the analysis as a basis for identifying appropriate and cost-effective measures as well as the determination of an acceptable level of risk

Attributes

Figure 49 describes attributes for security assessment services.

Figure 49—Security Assessment Services: Attributes

Service Capability	Supporting Technology	Benefit
Perform information security assessments.	• Vulnerability scanner • Fuzzers, sniffers • Protocol analysers • Passive and active network analysers • Honeypots • Endpoint agents • Application scanners • Compliance management • Reporting tools • Remote access (if needed), network, side channels, virtual private networks (VPNs)	• Identification of information security vulnerabilities • Identification of gaps that could lead to compliance issues
Perform information risk assessments.	• Same as above: • Vulnerability scanner • Fuzzers, sniffers • Protocol analysers • Log analyser • Passive and active network analysers • Honeypots • Endpoint agents • Application scanners • Compliance management • Reporting tools • Remote access (if needed), network, side channels, VPNs	• Provision of risk rating for information security practices • Help in prioritising vulnerabilities based on risk • Insight into ways to mitigate risk based on business needs

Goals

Figure 50 describes goals for security assessment services.

Figure 50—Security Assessment Services: Goals

Service Capability	Quality Goal	Metric
Perform information security assessments.	Accurate identification of all information security weaknesses, deficiencies, exposures, vulnerabilities and threats to a given asset or entity	Number of items discovered via incidents not covered in report
Perform information risk assessments.	Accurate identification of all information risk and resulting business risk/effects to a given asset or entity	Areas of new risk discovered via incidents not covered in report

F.5 Adequately Secured and Configured Systems, Aligned With Security Requirements and Security Architecture

Description of the Service Capability

Figure 51 describes the service capability for adequately secured systems services.

Figure 51—Adequately Secured Systems Services: Description of the Service Capability

Service Capability	Description
Provide adequately secured hardened and configured systems, in line with information security requirements and information security architecture.	Provide the information security-related configuration, settings and system hardening to ensure that the information security posture of a given system is based on a set of requirements or architectural designs.
Provide device information security protection.	Provide device-specific information security measures and activities.
Provide physical information protection.	Provide adequate, specific information security measures for data and information that exist in non-digital forms, including documents, media, facilities, physical perimeter and transit.

Attributes

Figure 52 describes attributes for adequately secured systems services.

Figure 52—Adequately Secured Systems Services: Attributes

Service Capability	Supporting Technology	Benefit
Provide adequately secured hardened and configured systems, in line with information security requirements and information security architecture.	• File Transfer Protocol (FTP) • CMDB update methods • Signature verification solutions • File integrity monitoring • Kernel modules • Information security requirements and information security architecture • System management • Patch management • Virtualisation management • Cloud management	• Reduced unauthorised access to data • Reduced external and internal threats • Simplified compliance
Provide device information security protection.	• Device-specific platform OS • Platform management console/systems	• Confidentiality in case of theft • Prevention of unauthorised access to specific devices • More explicit information security for specific devices
Provide physical information protection.	• Closed-circuit television (CCTV) • Locks • Alarms • Access control • Vaulting • Intelligence reports • First responder interfaces • Facilities management solutions • Fire protection systems • Time locks • Physical access solutions	• Protection of physical assets from external and internal threats

Goals

Figure 53 describes goals for adequately secured systems services.

Figure 53—Adequately Secured Systems Services: Goals

Service Capability	Quality Goal	Metric
Provide adequately secured hardened and configured systems, in line with information security requirements and information security architecture.	Improvements in information security configuration of systems in alignment with information security requirements	Number of information security issues discovered after an information security assessment of the hardened system
Provide device information security protection.	Improvements in information security configuration of device in alignment with information security requirements	Number of information security issues discovered after an information security assessment of the secured device
Provide physical information protection.	Physical controls in line with information security requirements	Number of incidents not discovered by review/ assessment
		Number incidents detected not addressed by existing controls

F.6 User Access and Access Rights in Line With Business Requirements

Description of the Service Capability

Figure 54 describes the service capability for user access and access rights services.

Figure 54—User Access and Access Rights Services: Description of the Service Capability

Service Capability	Description
Provide authentication services.	Provide a set of capabilities for performing user or entity identification using a set of factors as determined by the information security policy or access control requirements.
Provide information security provisioning services.	Provide a set of capabilities for creating, delivering and managing the information security-enabling technologies to a given system, entity, application, service or device.

(continued)

Figure 54—User Access and Access Rights Services: Description of the Service Capability

Service Capability	Description
Evaluate information security entity classification services.	Evaluate the categories, classification, information security level and sensitivity for a given entity, system, process, procedure, application, service or organisational unit.
Provide revocation services.	Provide a set of capabilities for cancelling, withdrawing or terminating information security rights or abilities for a given system, entity, application, service, process, procedure, organisational unit or device.
Provide user authentication and authorisation rights in line with business requirements.	Provide a set of capabilities and management practices for performing user identification using a set of factors as determined by the information security policy or access control requirements as defined by the business requirements.

Attributes

Figure 55 describes attributes for user access and access rights services.

Figure 55—User Access and Access Rights Services: Attributes

Service Capability	Supporting Technology	Benefit
Provide authentication services.	• Biometrics • Certificates • Dongles • Smart cards • Embedded device IDs • One-time passwords (OTPs), fobs, cellular telephones • Username/passwords • Identity as a Service (IDaaS), barcodes, universal • product code (UPC) • Certificate revocation list (CRL), ID federation • Root certificates • Key management services • Location services • Reputation services • Public key infrastructure (PKI)	• Prevention of unauthorised access to systems/data • Assurance that every entity has only the necessary level of access • Safeguarding of sensitive information • Verification of the identity of users accessing systems

(continued)

Figure 55—User Access and Access Rights Services: Attributes

Service Capability	Supporting Technology	Benefit
Provide information security provisioning services.	• Open Mobile Alliance (OMA) Device Management (DM) provisioning • Subscriber identity module (SIM), certificates, root certificates • Local and remote encryption services • Key management services • Location services system and device Management solutions • Software distribution solutions • HR data feed	Appropriate and timely access to needed systems for employees
Provide information security entity classification services.	• Diagram and visualisation tools • Classification tools • CMDB • Enterprise architecture • Classification standards • Release candidate push solutions	Enables appropriate grouping and categorisation of information security entities to classify the appropriate level of risk
Provide revocation services.	• SIM, certificates, root certificates • Local and remote encryption services • Key management services • Location services • HR data feed • PKI	• Prevention of systems access by unauthorised users • after their privileges have been revoked (due to termination or role change) • Reduced likelihood of an internal attack
Provide user authentication and authorisation rights in line with business requirements.	• SIM, certificates, root certificates • Local and remote encryption services • Key management services • Location services • PKI	• Verification that users have appropriate level of access to needed systems only • Reduced exposure of sensitive data • Reduced likelihood of internal attack

Goals

Figure 56 describes goals for user access and access rights services.

Figure 56—User Access and Access Rights Services: Goals		
Service Capability	Quality Goal	Metric
Provide authentication services.	Accurate, complete and timely authentication of all entities and/or services	• Number of entities or services not under the authentication service • Completeness of authentication factors supporting information security requirements
Provide information security provisioning services.	Accurate, complete and timely provisioning of all services and information security elements for entities, devices or services	• Number of incomplete provisioning transactions • Number of inaccurate provisioning transactions • Average delay in provision • Violation of maximum delay in provisioning
Provide information security entity classification services.	Accurate and complete classification of all entities	• Number of inaccuracies in classification • Number of classes not defined for entities discovered • Number of changes required to existing classifications
Provide revocation privilege services.	Accurate, complete, and timely revocation of all entities and/or services	• Number of failed revocations for targets • Completeness of revocations supporting information security requirements • Delay in revocation of entities and services for a given target
Provide user authentication and authorisation rights in line with business requirements.	Accurate, complete, and timely authentication and proper authorisation of all entities and/or services	• Number of entities or services not under the authentication or authorisation service • Completeness of authentication and authorisation factors supporting information security and business requirements

F.7 Adequate Protection Against Malware, External Attacks and Intrusion Attempts

Description of the Service Capability

Figure 57 describes the service capability for protection against malware and attacks services.

Figure 57—Protection Against Malware and Attacks Services: Description of the Service Capability

Service Capability	Description
Provide information security and countermeasures for threats (internal and external).	Plan, implement, maintain and improve measures, countermeasures and activities including, but not limited to, actions, processes, devices or systems, addressing threats and vulnerabilities as identified in the risk assessments, information security policies and information security strategy.
	Remain up to date on emerging technologies.
Provide data protection (in host, network, cloud and storage).	Provide a set of capabilities and management practices for implementing protection, confidentiality, integrity and availability of data in all of their states including, but not limited to, at rest or in transit, locally and externally, short-term and long-term.

Attributes

Figure 58 describes attributes for protection against malware and attacks services.

Figure 58—Protection Against Malware and Attacks Services: Attributes		
Service Capability	Supporting Technology	Benefit
Provide information security and countermeasures for threats (internal and external).	• Encryption • PKI, deep packet inspection (DPI), sniffers • Firewalls • Packet analyser, sensors • Compliance management • Information security requirements and information security architecture • CMDB • System patch management • Virtualisation management • Cloud management • Vendor-supplied dashboards and management agents • Vendor-supplied updates • Open source software (OSS) repositories • Vendor information security advisories and KBs, honeypots, tarpits • Antimalware, antirootkit, antispyware, antiphishing • Browser protection, sandboxing, content inspection • Reputation services	• An up-to-date reference for remediating threats • Prevention of internal and external attacks

(*continued*)

Figure 58—Protection Against Malware and Attacks Services: Attributes		
Service Capability	Supporting Technology	Benefit
Provide data protection (in host, network, cloud and storage).	• PKI, sniffers, DPI • Encryption services • Data loss prevention (DLP) • System and device management solutions • Software distribution solutions • Remote management systems • Virtualisation and cloud management solutions • Document management • Data classification systems • Application-centric data management solutions • Data obfuscation solutions	• Ability for data to be stored and transferred securely • Confidentiality, integrity and availability

Goals

Figure 59 describes goals for protection against malware and attacks services.

Figure 59—Protection Against Malware and Attacks Services: Goals		
Service Capability	Quality Goal	Metric
Provide information security and countermeasures for threats (internal and external).	Maximised protection against known and unknown threats	Number of information security-related incidents
Provide data protection (in host, network, cloud and storage).	Maximised data protection for all data states	Number of data exposures

APPENDIX B

■ ■ ■

Experian EI3PA Security Assessment

This appendix contains excerpts from Experian's EI3PA Security Assessment standard that are most applicable to web application security. EI3PA is available directly from Experian and is not published on the Experian web site.

The material is this appendix is provided with copyright permission from Experian and from PCI.

Experian sublicenses content from PCI, so copyright permissions from both organizations are included.

Portions of this production are provided courtesy of PCI Security Standards Council, LLC ("PCI SSC") and/or its licensors, and are protected by copyright laws. All rights reserved. Neither PCI SSC nor its licensors endorses this production, its providers or the methods, procedures, statements, views, opinions or advice contained herein. All references to documents, materials or portions thereof provided by PCI SSC should be read as qualified by the actual materials made available by PCI SSC. For questions regarding such materials, please contact PCI SSC through its web site at https://www.pcisecuritystandards.org.

Portions included within the PCI SSC materials in this production are copyrighted by Experian Information Solutions, Inc. All rights reserved. Experian is the registered trademark of Experian Information Solutions, Inc.

Requirement 2: Do not use vendor-supplied defaults for system passwords and other security parameters for systems housing or processing Experian provided data.

Malicious individuals (external and internal to a company) often use vendor default passwords and other vendor default settings to compromise systems. These passwords and settings are well known in hacker communities and easily determined via public information.

Requirements	Testing Procedures
2.1 Always change vendor-supplied defaults before installing a system on the network, including but not limited to passwords, simple network management protocol (SNMP) community strings, and elimination of unnecessary accounts.	**2.1** Choose a sample of system components, and attempt to log on (with system administrator help) to the devices using default vendor-supplied accounts and passwords, to verify that default accounts and passwords have been changed. (Use vendor manuals and sources on the Internet to find vendor-supplied accounts/passwords.)
2.2 Develop configuration standards for all system components. Assure that these standards address all known security vulnerabilities and are consistent with industry-accepted system hardening standards. Sources of industry-accepted system hardening standards may include, but are not limited to: • Center for Internet Security (CIS) • International Organization for Standardization (ISO) • SysAdmin Audit Network Security (SANS) Institute • National Institute of Standards Technology (NIST)	**2.2.a** Examine the organization's system configuration standards for all types of system components and verify the system configuration standards are consistent with industry- accepted hardening standards. **2.2.b** Verify that system configuration standards are updated as new vulnerability issues are identified, as defined in Requirement 6.2. **2.2.c** Verify that system configuration standards are applied when new systems are configured. **2.2.d** Verify that system configuration standards include each item below (2.2.1 – 2.2.4).
2.2.2 Enable only necessary and secure services, protocols, daemons, etc., as required for the function of the system. Implement security features for any required services, protocols or daemons that are considered to be insecure—for example, use secured technologies such as SSH, S-FTP, SSL, or IPSec VPN to protect insecure services such as NetBIOS, file-sharing, Telnet, FTP, etc.	**2.2.2.a** For a sample of system components, inspect enabled system services, daemons, and protocols. Verify that only necessary services or protocols are enabled. **2.2.2.b** Identify any enabled insecure services, daemons, or protocols. Verify they are justified and that security features are documented and implemented.

(*continued*)

Requirement 2: Do not use vendor-supplied defaults for system passwords and other security parameters for systems housing or processing Experian provided data.

2.2.4 Remove all unnecessary functionality, such as scripts, drivers, features, subsystems, file systems, and unnecessary web servers.

2.2.4.a For a sample of system components, verify that all unnecessary functionality (for example, scripts, drivers, features, subsystems, file systems, etc.) is removed.

2.2.4.b. Verify enabled functions are documented and support secure configuration.

2.2.4.c. Verify that only documented functionality is present on the sampled system components.

2.3 Encrypt all non-console administrative access using strong cryptography. Use technologies such as SSH, VPN, or SSL/TLS for web-based management and other non-console administrative access.

2.3 For a sample of system components, verify that non-console administrative access is encrypted by performing the following:

2.3.a Observe an administrator log on to each system to verify that a strong encryption method is invoked before the administrator's password is requested.

2.3.b Review services and parameter files on systems to determine that Telnet and other remote login commands are not available for use internally.

2.3.c Verify that administrator access to the web-based management interfaces is encrypted with strong cryptography.

149

Requirement 4: Encrypt transmission of Experian provided data across public networks.

Sensitive information must be encrypted during transmission over networks that are easily accessed by malicious individuals. Misconfigured wireless networks and vulnerabilities in legacy encryption and authentication protocols continue to be targets of malicious individuals who exploit these vulnerabilities to gain privileged access to Experian provided data environments.

Requirements	Testing Procedures
4.1 Use strong cryptography and security protocols (for example, SSL/TLS, IPSEC, SSH, etc.) to safeguard sensitive Experian provided data during transmission over open, public networks. Examples of open, public networks that are in scope of the PCI DSS include but are not limited to: • The Internet • Wireless technologies, • Global System for Mobile communications (GSM) • General Packet Radio Service (GPRS)	**4.1** Verify the use of security protocols wherever Experian provided data is transmitted or received over open, public networks. Verify that strong cryptography is used during data transmission, as follows: **4.1.a** Select a sample of transactions as they are received and observe transactions as they occur to verify that Experian provided data is encrypted during transit. **4.1.b** Verify that only trusted keys and/or certificates are accepted. **4.1.c** Verify that the protocol is implemented to use only secure configurations, and does not support insecure versions or configurations. **4.1.d** Verify that the proper encryption strength is implemented for the encryption methodology in use. (Check vendor recommendations/best practices.) **4.1.e** For SSL/TLS implementations: • Verify that HTTPS appears as a part of the browser Universal Record Locator (URL). • Verify that no Experian provided data is required when HTTPS does not appear in the URL.

Requirement 5: Use and regularly update anti-virus software for systems housing, accessing or processing Experian provided data.

Malicious software, commonly referred to as —malware—including viruses, worms, and Trojans—enters the network during many business-approved activities including employee e-mail and use of the Internet, mobile computers, and storage devices, resulting in the exploitation of system vulnerabilities. Anti-virus software must be used on all systems commonly affected by malware to protect systems from current and evolving malicious software threats.

Requirements	Testing Procedures
5.1 Deploy anti-virus software on all systems commonly affected by malicious software (particularly personal computers and servers).	**5.1** For a sample of system components including all operating system types commonly affected by malicious software, verify that anti-virus software is deployed if applicable anti-virus technology exists.
5.1.1 Ensure that all anti-virus programs are capable of detecting, removing, and protecting against all known types of malicious software.	**5.1.1** For a sample of system components, verify that all anti-virus programs detect, remove, and protect against all known types of malicious software (for example, viruses, Trojans, worms, spyware, adware, and rootkits).
5.2 Ensure that all anti-virus mechanisms are current, and actively running, and capable of generating audit logs.	**5.2** Verify that all anti-virus software is current, actively running, and generating logs by performing the following: **5.2.a** Obtain and examine the policy and verify that it requires updating of anti-virus software and definitions. **5.2.b** Verify that the master installation of the software is enabled for automatic updates and periodic scans.

151

Requirement 6: Develop and maintain secure systems and applications.

Unscrupulous individuals use security vulnerabilities to gain privileged access to systems. Many of these vulnerabilities are fixed by vendor-provided security patches, which must be installed by the entities that manage the systems. All critical systems must have the most recently released, appropriate software patches to protect against exploitation and compromise of Experian provided data by malicious individuals and malicious software. Note: Appropriate software patches are those patches that have been evaluated and tested sufficiently to determine that the patches do not conflict with existing security configurations. For in-house developed applications, numerous vulnerabilities can be avoided by using standard system development processes and secure coding techniques.

Requirements	Testing Procedures
6.1 Ensure that all system components and software are protected from known vulnerabilities by having the latest vendor- supplied security patches installed. Install critical security patches within one month of release.	**6.1.a** For a sample of system components and related software, compare the list of security patches installed on each system to the most recent vendor security patch list, to verify that current vendor patches are installed
Note: An organization may consider applying a risk-based approach to prioritize their patch installations. For example, by prioritizing critical infrastructure (for example, public-facing devices and systems, databases) higher than less-critical internal devices, to ensure high-priority systems and devices are addressed within one month, and addressing less critical devices and systems within three months	**6.1.b** Examine policies related to security patch installation to verify they require installation of all critical new security patches within one month.
6.2 Establish a process to identify and assign a risk ranking to newly discovered security vulnerabilities.	**6.2.a** Interview responsible personnel to verify that processes are implemented to identify new security vulnerabilities, and that a risk ranking is assigned to such vulnerabilities. (At minimum, the most critical, highest risk vulnerabilities should be ranked as "High".
Notes:	
• Risk rankings should be based on industry best practices. For example, criteria for ranking "High" risk vulnerabilities m ay include a CVSS base score of 4.0 or above, and/or a vendor-supplied patch classified by the vendor as "critical," and/or a vulnerability affecting a critical system component.	**6.2.b** Verify that processes to identify new security vulnerabilities include using outside sources for security vulnerability information.
• The ranking of vulnerabilities as defined in 6.2.a is considered a best practice until June 30, 2012, after which it becomes a requirement.	

(continued)

Requirement 6: Develop and maintain secure systems and applications.

6.3 Develop software applications (internal and external, and including web-based administrative access to applications) in accordance with PCI DSS (for example, secure authentication and logging), and based on industry best practices. Incorporate information security throughout the software development life cycle. These processes must include the following:

6.3.a Obtain and examine written software development processes to verify that the processes are based on industry standards and/or best practices and accordance with PCI DSS

6.3.b Examine written software development processes to verify that information security is included throughout the life cycle

6.3.c Examine written software development processes to verify that software applications are developed in accordance with PCI DSS.

6.3.d From an examination of written software development processes, and interviews of software developers, verify that:

6.3.1 Removal of custom application accounts, user IDs, and passwords before applications become active or are released to customers.

6.3.1 Custom application accounts, user IDs and/or passwords are removed before system goes into production or is released to customers.

6.3.2 Review of custom code prior to release to production or customers in order to identify any potential coding vulnerability.

Note: This requirement for code reviews applies to all custom code (both internal and public-facing), as part of the system development life cycle.

Code reviews can be conducted by knowledgeable internal personnel or third parties. Web applications are also subject to additional controls, if they are public facing, to address ongoing threats and vulnerabilities after implementation, as defined at PCI DSS Requirement 6.6

6.3.2.a Obtain and review policies to confirm that all custom application code changes must be reviewed (using either manual or automated processes) as follows:

- Code changes are reviewed by individuals other than the originating code author, and by individuals who are knowledgeable in code review techniques and secure coding practices.

- Code reviews ensure code is developed according to secure coding guidelines (see PCI DSS Requirement 6.5).

- Appropriate corrections are implemented prior to release.

- Code review results are reviewed and approved by management prior to release.

(*continued*)

Requirement 6: Develop and maintain secure systems and applications.

6.4 Follow change control processes and procedures for all changes to system components. The processes must include the following:

6.4 From an examination of change control processes, interviews with system and network administrators, and examination of relevant data (network configuration documentation, production and test data, etc.), verify the following:

6.4.1 Separate development/test and production environments.

6.4.1 The development/test environments are separate from the production environment, with access control in place to enforce the separation.

6.4.2 Separation of duties between development/test and production environments.

6.4.2 There is a separation of duties between personnel assigned to the development/test environments and those assigned to the production environment.

6.4.3 Production data (consumer data) are not used for testing or development.

6.4.3 Production data (consumer) are not used for testing or development.

6.4.4 Removal of test data and accounts before production systems become active.

6.4.4 Test data and accounts are removed before a production system becomes active.

6.4.5 Change control procedures for the implementation of security patches and software modifications. Procedures must include the following:

6.4.5.a Verify that change-control procedures related to implementing security patches and software modifications are documented and require items 6.4.5.1 – 6.4.5.4 below.

6.4.5.1 Documentation of impact.

6.4.5.1 Verify that documentation of impact is included in the change control documentation for each sampled change.

6.4.5.2 Documented change approval by authorized parties.

6.4.5.2 Verify that documented approval by authorized parties is present for each sampled change.

6.4.5.3 Functionality testing to verify that the change does not adversely impact the security of the system.

6.4.5.3.a For each sampled change, verify that functionality testing is performed to verify that the change does not adversely impact the security of the system.

6.4.5.3.b For custom code changes, verify that all updates are tested for compliance with PCI DSS Requirement 6.5 before being deployed into production.

6.4.5.4 Back-out procedures.

6.4.5.4 Verify that back-out procedures are prepared for each sampled change.

(*continued*)

Requirement 6: Develop and maintain secure systems and applications.

6.5 Develop applications based on secure coding guidelines.

Prevent common coding vulnerabilities in software development processes, to include the following:

Note: The vulnerabilities listed at 6.5.1 through 6.5.9 were current with industry best practices when this version of PCI DSS was published. However, as industry best practices for vulnerability management are updated (for example, the OWASP Guide, SANS CWE Top 25, CERT Secure Coding, etc.), the current best practices must be used for these requirements.

6.5.a Obtain and review software development processes.

Verify that processes require training in secure coding techniques for developers, based on industry best practices and guidance.

6.5.b. Verify that processes are in place to ensure that applications are not vulnerable to, at a minimum, the following:

6.5.1 Injection flaws, particularly SQL injection. Also consider OS Command Injection, LDAP and XPath injection flaws as well as other injection flaws.

6.5.1 Injection flaws, particularly SQL injection. (Validate input to verify user data cannot modify meaning of commands and queries, utilize parameterized queries, etc.)

6.5.2 Buffer overflow.

6.5.2 Buffer overflow (Validate buffer boundaries and truncate input strings).

6.5.3 Insecure cryptographic storage.

6.5.3 Insecure cryptographic storage (Prevent cryptographic flaws).

6.5.4 Insecure communications.

6.5.4 Insecure communications (Properly encrypt all authenticated and sensitive communications).

6.5.5 Improper error handling.

6.5.5 Improper error handling (Do not leak information via error messages).

6.5.6 All "High" vulnerabilities identified in the vulnerability identification process (as defined in PCI DSS Requirement 6.2).

Note: This requirement is considered a best practice until June 30, 2012, after which it becomes a requirement.

6.5.6 All "High" vulnerabilities as identified in PCI DSS Requirement 6.2.

(continued)

155

Requirement 6: Develop and maintain secure systems and applications.

6.6 For public-facing web applications, address new threats and vulnerabilities on an ongoing basis and ensure these applications are protected against known attacks by either of the following methods:

- Reviewing public-facing web applications via manual or automated application vulnerability security assessment tools or methods, at least annually and after any changes
- Installing a web-application firewall in front of public-facing web applications

6.6 For public-facing web applications, ensure that either one of the following methods are in place as follows:

- Verify that public-facing web applications are reviewed (using either manual or automated vulnerability security assessment tools or methods), as follows:
  - At least annually
  - After any changes
  - By an organization or in-house subject matter experts that specializes in application security
  - That all vulnerabilities are corrected
  - That the application is re-evaluated after the corrections
- Verify that a web-application firewall is in place in front of public-facing web applications to detect and prevent web-based attacks.

Note: *"An organization that specializes in application Security" can be either a third-party company or an internal organization, as long as the reviewers specialize in application security and can demonstrate independence from the development team verify that a web-application firewall is in place in front of public-facing web applications to detect and prevent web-based attacks.*

Requirement 10: Track and monitor all access to network resources and Experian provided data.

Logging mechanisms and the ability to track user activities are critical in preventing, detecting, or minimizing the impact of a data compromise. The presence of logs in all environments allows thorough tracking, alerting, and analysis when something does go wrong. Determining the cause of a compromise is very difficult, if not impossible, without system activity logs.

Requirements	Testing Procedures
10.1 Establish a process for linking all access to system components (especially access done with administrative privileges such as root) to each individual user.	**10.1** Verify through observation and interviewing the system administrator, that audit trails are enabled and active for system components.
10.2 Implement automated audit trails for all system components to reconstruct the following events:	**10.2** Through interviews, examination of audit logs, and examination of audit log settings, perform the following:
10.2.1 All individual accesses to Experian provided data.	**10.2.1** Verify all individual access to Experian provided data is logged.
10.2.2 All actions taken by any individual with root or administrative privileges.	**10.2.2** Verify actions taken by any individual with root or administrative privileges are logged.
10.2.3 Access to all audit trails.	**10.2.3** Verify access to all audit trails is logged.
10.2.4 Invalid logical access attempts.	**10.2.4** Verify invalid logical access attempts are logged.
10.2.5 Use of identification and authentication mechanisms.	**10.2.5** Verify use of identification and authentication mechanisms is logged.
10.2.6 Initialization of the audit logs.	**10.2.6** Verify initialization of audit logs is logged.
10.2.7 Creation and deletion of system-level objects.	**10.2.7** Verify creation and deletion of system level objects are logged.
10.3 Record at least the following audit trail entries for all system components for each event:	**10.3** Through interviews and observation, for each auditable event (from 10.2), perform the following:
10.3.1 User identification.	**10.3.1** Verify user identification is included in log entries.
10.3.2 Type of event.	**10.3.2** Verify type of event is included in log entries.
10.3.3 Date and time.	**10.3.3** Verify date and time stamp is included in log entries.

(continued)

Requirement 10: Track and monitor all access to network resources and Experian provided data.

10.3.4 Success or failure indication.	**10.3.4** Verify success or failure indication is included in log entries.
10.3.5 Origination of event.	**10.3.5** Verify origination of event is included in log entries.
10.3.6 Identity or name of affected data, system component, or resource.	**10.3.6** Verify identity or name of affected data, system component, or resources is included in log entries.

Requirement 11: Regularly test security systems and processes.

Vulnerabilities are continually being discovered by malicious individuals and researchers, and being introduced by new software. Systems, components, processes, and custom software should be tested frequently to ensure security controls continue to reflect a changing environment.

Requirements	**Testing Procedures**
11.2.1 Perform quarterly internal vulnerability scans.	**11.2.1.a** Review the scan reports and verify that four quarterly internal scans occurred in the most recent 12-month period.
	11.2.1.b Review the scan reports and verify that the scan process includes rescans until passing results are obtained, or all "High" vulnerabilities.
	11.2.1.c Validate that the scan was performed by a qualified internal resource(s) or qualified external third party, and if applicable, organizational independence of the tester exists (not required to be a QSA or ASV).

(continued)

Requirement 11: Regularly test security systems and processes.

11.2.2 Perform quarterly external vulnerability scans via an Approved Scanning Vendor (ASV), approved by the Payment Card Industry Security Standards Council (PCI SSC).

Note: Quarterly external vulnerability scans must be performed by an Approved Scanning Vendor (ASV), approved by the Payment Card Industry Security Standards Council (PCI SSC). Scans conducted after network changes may be performed by internal staff.

11.2.2.a Review output from the four most recent quarters of external vulnerability scans and verify that four quarterly scans occurred in the most recent 12-month period.

11.2.2.b Review the results of each quarterly scan to ensure that they satisfy the ASV Program Guide requirements (for example, no vulnerabilities rated higher than a 4.0 by the CVSS and no automatic failures).

11.2.2.c Review the scan reports to verify that the scans were completed by an Approved Scanning Vendor (ASV), approved by the PCI SSC.

11.3 Perform penetration testing on network infrastructure and applications at least once a year, and after any significant infrastructure or application upgrade or modification (e.g., operating system upgrade, sub-network added to environment, web server added to environment).

11.3 Obtain results from the most recent penetration test to verify that penetration testing is performed at least annually and after any significant changes to the environment. Confirm that any noted vulnerabilities were corrected.

APPENDIX C

ISO/IEC 17799:2005 and the ISO/IEC 27000:2014 Series

The material in this appendix is taken from the ISO (International Organization for Standardization) web site sections pertaining to information security. I have included it as a convenient compliance resource because it is referred to in Chapter 8 and other places throughout the book and is highly regarded. Having said that, its inclusion is more for completeness than for any significant contribution to web application security vulnerability knowledge. Even the most closely related ISO standards do not go into detail about web application security.

Specifically, this appendix includes summary outlines of the ISO/IEC 17799:2005 guidelines and the ISO 27000:2014 family of standards. Of the subject material published by the ISO, ISO/IEC 17799:2005 is the most closely related to web application security. The ISO/IEC 27000:2014 series is a family of standards useful for security framework planning.

ISO/IEC 17799:2005

As a quick point of reference, I have included an outline of the most current contents of ISO/IEC 17799:2005. Although it does not include any specific reference to web application security, this standard is an important set of guidelines and best practices. As such, it is not technical and is technology agnostic.

Note For detailed information on ISO/IEC 17799:2005, please visit the ISO information technology page for "Security techniques – Code of practice for information security management" at www.iso.org/iso/iso_catalogue/catalogue_ics/catalogue_detail_ics.htm?csnumber=39612.

The topics covered by ISO/IEC 17799:2005 include the following:

- Security policy
- Organization of information security
- Asset management
- Human resources security
- Physical and environmental security
- Communications and operations management
- Access control
- Information systems acquisition, development, and maintenance
- Information security incident management
- Business continuity management
- Compliance

The ISO/IEC 27000:2014 Series

The ISO also publishes several other IT security guidelines. These guidelines are most useful for security framework planning, though they are not specifically focused on web application security. This section includes a summary outline of the ISO information technology guidelines for "Security techniques: Information security management systems."

■ **Note**   For detailed information on the ISO 27000:2014 series, see the following page:
www.iso.org/iso/home/store/catalogue_tc/catalogue_detail.htm?csnumber=63411.

The ISO 27000:2014 family of standards includes:

- ISO/IEC 27000, Information security management systems — Overview and vocabulary
- ISO/IEC 27001, Information security management systems — Requirements
- ISO/IEC 27002, Code of practice for information security controls
- ISO/IEC 27003, Information security management system implementation guidance
- ISO/IEC 27004, Information security management — Measurement
- ISO/IEC 27005, Information security risk management

- ISO/IEC 27006, Requirements for bodies providing audit and certification of information security management systems

- ISO/IEC 27007, Guidelines for information security management systems auditing

- ISO/IEC TR 27008, Guidelines for auditors on information security controls

- ISO/IEC 27010, Information security management for inter-sector and inter-organizational communications

- ISO/IEC 27011, Information security management guidelines for telecommunications organizations based on ISO/IEC 27002

- ISO/IEC 27013, Guidance on the integrated implementation of ISO/IEC 27001 and ISO/IEC 20000-1

- ISO/IEC 27014, Governance of information security

- ISO/IEC TR 27015, Information security management guidelines for financial services

- ISO/IEC TR 27016, Information security management — Organizational economics

APPENDIX D

■ ■ ■

North American Energy Council Security Standard for Critical Infrastructure Protection (NERC CIP)

The material in this appendix is from the NERC CIP web page. I have included it as a convenient compliance resource since it is referred to in Chapter 8 and several places throughout the book.

The information is reproduced verbatim from the publications of the NERC CIP. The references within the material include mention of footnotes, related information, and other references to NERC documents. For clarity, these references are internal to NERC documentation and not to this book. Since this is copyrighted information, I have not made any changes whatsoever.

This appendix contains three major elements:

1. **NERC CIP Standards Currently in Force**: The sections of the NERC CIP standard that are currently in force.

2. **Future NERC CIP Standards**: The sections of the NERC CIP standard that will be enforced in the future and are currently works in progress by the NERC CIP standards council.

3. **Future Standard CIP-007-5: Cyber Security—System Security Management**: This document is a drill-down of excerpts from a work in progress called the "CIP 007-5: Cyber Security — System Security Management," which will be enforced in the future. This portion of the standards contains excellent recommendations pertaining to the security of any application environment.

■ **Note**   Complete information about the NERC CIP standards is available at
www.nerc.com/pa/Stand/Pages/CIPStandards.aspx.

NERC CIP Standards Currently in Force

Subject to Enforcement

CIP-002-3	Cyber Security — Critical Cyber Asset Identification
CIP-003-3	Cyber Security — Security Management Controls
CIP-004-3a	Cyber Security — Personnel & Training
CIP-005-3a	Cyber Security — Electronic Security Perimeter(s)
CIP-006-3c	Cyber Security — Physical Security of Critical Cyber Assets
CIP-007-3a	Cyber Security — Systems Security Management
CIP-008-3	Cyber Security — Incident Reporting and Response Planning
CIP-009-3	Cyber Security — Recovery Plans for Critical Cyber Assets
CIP-002-3	Cyber Security — Critical Cyber Asset Identification

Future NERC CIP Standards

Subject to Future Enforcement

CIP-002-5.1	Cyber Security — BES Cyber System Categorization
CIP-003-5	Cyber Security — Security Management Controls
CIP-004-5.1	Cyber Security — Personnel & Training
CIP-005-5	Cyber Security — Electronic Security Perimeter(s)
CIP-006-5	Cyber Security — Physical Security of BES Cyber Systems
CIP-007-5	Cyber Security — System Security Management
CIP-008-5	Cyber Security — Incident Reporting and Response Planning
CIP-009-5	Cyber Security — Recovery Plans for BES Cyber Systems
CIP-010-1	Cyber Security — Configuration Change Management and Vulnerability Assessments
CIP-011-1	Cyber Security — Information Protection

Future Standard CIP-007-5: Cyber Security — System Security Management

The material in this section provides details about the CIP-007-5 standard, excerpted with NERC permission from "CIP-007-5—Cyber Security – System Security Management".

■ **Note**   The full document for CIP-007-5 is available at `http://tinyurl.com/o6kj5uz`.

---

1. **Title:** Cyber Security — System Security Management

2. **Number:** CIP-007-5

3. **Purpose:** To manage system security by specifying select technical, operational, and procedural requirements in support of protecting BES Cyber Systems against compromise that could lead to misoperation or instability in the BES.

   ...

Requirement R1:

Requirement R1 exists to reduce the attack surface of Cyber Assets by requiring entities to disable known unnecessary ports. The SDT intends for the entity to know what network accessible ("listening") ports and associated services are accessible on their assets and systems, whether they are needed for that Cyber Asset's function, and disable or restrict access to all other ports.

1.1. This requirement is most often accomplished by disabling the corresponding service or program that is listening on the port or configuration settings within the Cyber Asset. It can also be accomplished through using host-based firewalls, TCP_Wrappers, or other means on the Cyber Asset to restrict access. Note that the requirement is applicable at the Cyber Asset level. The Cyber Assets are those which comprise the applicable BES Cyber Systems and their associated Cyber Assets. This control is another layer in the defense against network-based attacks, therefore the SDT intends that the control be on the device itself, or positioned inline in a non-bypassable manner. Blocking ports at the ESP border does not substitute for this device level requirement. If a device has no provision for disabling or restricting logical ports on the device (example - purpose built devices that run from firmware with no port configuration available) then those ports that are open are deemed 'needed'.

1.2. Examples of physical I/O ports include network, serial and USB ports external to the device casing. BES Cyber Systems should exist within a Physical Security Perimeter in which case the physical I/O ports have protection from unauthorized access, but it may still be possible for accidental use such as connecting a modem, connecting a network cable that bridges networks, or inserting a USB drive. Ports used for 'console commands' primarily means serial ports on Cyber Assets that provide an administrative interface. The protection of these ports can be accomplished in several ways including, but not limited to:

- Disabling all unneeded physical ports within the Cyber Asset's configuration

- Prominent signage, tamper tape, or other means of conveying that the ports

- should not be used without proper authorization

- Physical port obstruction through removable locks

This is a 'defense in depth' type control and it is acknowledged that there are other layers of control (the PSP for one) that prevent unauthorized personnel from gaining physical access to these ports. Even with physical access, it has been pointed out there are other ways to circumvent the control. This control, with its inclusion of means such as signage, is not meant to be a preventative control against intruders. Signage is indeed a directive control, not a preventative one. However, with a defense-in-depth posture, different layers and types of controls are required throughout the standard with this providing another layer for depth in Control Center environments. Once physical access has been achieved through the other preventative and detective measures by authorized personnel, a directive control that outlines proper behavior as a last line of defense are appropriate in these highest risk areas. In essence, signage would be used to remind authorized users to "think before you plug anything into one of these systems" which is the intent. This control is not designed primarily for intruders, but for example the authorized employee who intends to plug his possibly infected smartphone into an operator console USB port to charge the battery.

Requirement R2:

The SDT's intent of Requirement R2 is to require entities to know, track, and mitigate the known software vulnerabilities associated with their BES Cyber Assets. It is not strictly an "install every security patch" requirement; the main intention is to "be aware of in a timely manner and manage all known vulnerabilities" requirement.

Patch management is required for BES Cyber Systems that are accessible remotely as well as standalone systems. Stand alone systems are vulnerable to intentional or unintentional introduction of malicious code. A sound defense-in-depth security strategy employs additional measures such as physical security, malware prevention software, and software patch management to reduce the introduction of malicious code or the exploit of known vulnerabilities.

One or multiple processes could be utilized. An overall assessment process may exist in a top tier document with lower tier documents establishing the more detailed process followed for individual systems. Lower tier documents could be used to cover BES Cyber System nuances that may occur at the system level.

2.1. The Responsible Entity is to have a patch management program that covers tracking, evaluating, and installing cyber security patches. The requirement applies to patches only, which are fixes released to handle a specific vulnerability in a hardware or software product. The requirement covers only patches that involve cyber security fixes and does not cover patches that are purely functionality related with no cyber security impact. Tracking involves processes for notification of the availability of new cyber security patches for the Cyber Assets. Documenting the patch source in the tracking portion of the process is required to determine when the assessment timeframe clock starts. This requirement handles the situation where security patches can come from an original source (such as an operating system vendor), but must be approved or certified by another source (such as a control system vendor) before they can be assessed and applied in order to not jeopardize the availability or integrity of the control system. The source can take many forms. The National Vulnerability Database, Operating System vendors, or Control System vendors could all be sources to monitor for release of security related patches, hotfixes, and/or updates. A patch source is not required for Cyber Assets that have no updateable software or firmware (there is no user accessible way to update the internal software or firmware executing on the Cyber Asset), or those Cyber Assets that have no existing source of patches such as vendors that no longer exist. The identification of these sources is intended to be performed once unless software is changed or added to the Cyber Asset's baseline.

2.2. Responsible Entities are to perform an assessment of security related patches within 35 days of release from their monitored source. An assessment should consist of determination of the applicability of each patch to the entity's specific environment and systems. Applicability determination is based primarily on whether the patch applies to a specific software or hardware component that the entity does have installed in an applicable Cyber Asset. A patch that applies to a service or component that is not installed in the entity's environment is not applicable. If the patch is determined to be non-applicable, that is documented with the reasons why and the entity is compliant. If the patch is applicable, the assessment can include a determination of the risk involved, how the vulnerability can be remediated, the urgency and timeframe of the remediation, and the steps the entity has previously taken or will take. Considerable care must be taken in applying security related patches, hotfixes, and/or updates or applying compensating measures to BES Cyber System or BES Cyber Assets that are no longer supported by vendors. It is possible security patches, hotfixes, and updates may reduce the reliability of the system, and entities should take this into account when determining the type of mitigation to apply. The Responsible Entities can use the information provided in the Department of Homeland Security "Quarterly Report on Cyber Vulnerabilities of Potential Risk to Control Systems" as a source. The DHS document "Recommended Practice for Patch Management of Control Systems" provides guidance on an evaluative process. It uses severity levels determined using the Common Vulnerability Scoring System Version 2. Determination that a security related patch, hotfix, and/or update poses too great a risk to install on a system or is not applicable due to the system configuration should not require a TFE.

When documenting the remediation plan measures it may not be necessary to document them on a one to one basis. The remediation plan measures may be cumulative. A measure to address a software vulnerability may involve disabling a particular service. That same service may be exploited through other software vulnerabilities. Therefore disabling the single service has addressed multiple patched vulnerabilities.

2.3. The requirement handles the situations where it is more of a reliability risk to patch a running system than the vulnerability presents. In all cases, the entity either installs the patch or documents (either through the creation of a new or update of an existing mitigation plan) what they are going to do to mitigate the vulnerability and when they are going to do so. There are times when it is in the best interest of reliability to not install a patch, and the entity can document what they have done to mitigate the vulnerability. For those security related patches that are determined to be applicable, the Responsible Entity must within 35 days either install the patch, create a dated mitigation plan which will outline the actions to be taken or those that have already been taken by the Responsible Entity to mitigate the vulnerabilities addressed by the security patch, or revise an existing mitigation plan. Timeframes do not have to be designated as a particular calendar day but can have event designations such as "at next scheduled outage of at least two days duration." "Mitigation plans" in the standard refers to internal documents and are not to be confused with plans that are submitted to Regional Entities in response to violations.

2.4. The entity has been notified of, has assessed, and has developed a plan to remediate the known risk and that plan must be implemented. Remediation plans that only include steps that have been previously taken are considered implemented upon completion of the documentation. Remediation plans that have steps to be taken to remediate the vulnerability must be implemented by the timeframe the entity documented in their plan. There is no maximum timeframe in this requirement as patching and other system changes carries its own risk to the availability and integrity of the systems and may require waiting until a planned outage. In periods of high demand or threatening weather, changes to systems may be curtailed or denied due to the risk to reliability.

Requirement R3:

3.1. Due to the wide range of equipment comprising the BES Cyber Systems and the wide variety of vulnerability and capability of that equipment to malware as well as the constantly evolving threat and resultant tools and controls, it is not practical within the standard to prescribe how malware is to be addressed on each Cyber Asset. Rather, the Responsible Entity determines on a BES Cyber System basis which Cyber Assets have susceptibility to malware intrusions and documents their plans and processes for addressing those risks and provides evidence that they follow those plans and processes. There are numerous options available including traditional antivirus solutions for common operating systems, white-listing solutions, network isolation techniques, portable storage media policies, Intrusion Detection/Prevention (IDS/IPS) solutions, etc. If an entity has numerous BES Cyber Systems or Cyber Assets that are of identical architecture, they may provide one process that describes how all the like Cyber Assets are covered. If a specific Cyber Asset has no updateable software and its executing code cannot be altered, then that Cyber Asset is considered to have its own internal method of deterring malicious code.

3.2. When malicious code is detected on a Cyber Asset within the applicability of this requirement, the threat posed by that code must be mitigated. In situations where traditional antivirus products are used, they may be configured to automatically remove or quarantine the malicious code. In white-listing situations, the white-listing tool itself can mitigate the threat as it will not allow the code to execute, however steps should still be taken to remove the malicious code from the Cyber Asset. In some instances, it may be in the best interest of reliability to not immediately remove or quarantine the malicious code, such as when availability of the system may be jeopardized by removal while operating and a rebuild of the system needs to be scheduled. In that case, monitoring may be increased and steps taken to insure the malicious code cannot communicate with other systems. In some instances the entity may be working with law enforcement or other governmental entities to closely monitor the code and track the perpetrator(s). For these reasons, there is no maximum timeframe or method prescribed for the removal of the malicious code, but the requirement is to mitigate the threat posed by the now identified malicious code.

3.3. In instances where malware detection technologies depend on signatures or patterns of known attacks, the effectiveness of these tools against evolving threats is tied to the ability to keep these signatures and patterns updated in a timely manner. The entity is to have a documented process that includes the testing and installation of signature or pattern updates. In a BES Cyber System, there may be some Cyber Assets that would benefit from the more timely installation of the updates where availability of that Cyber Asset would not jeopardize the availability of the BES Cyber System's ability to perform its function. For example, some HMI workstations where portable media is utilized may benefit from having the very latest updates at all times with minimal testing. Other Cyber Assets should have any updates thoroughly tested before implementation where the result of a 'false positive' could harm the availability of the BES Cyber System. The testing should not negatively impact the reliability of the BES. The testing should be focused on the update itself and if it will have an adverse impact on the BES Cyber System. Testing in no way implies that the entity is testing to ensure that malware is indeed detected by introducing malware into the environment. It is strictly focused on ensuring that the update does not negatively impact the BES Cyber System before those updates are placed into production.

Requirement R4:

Refer to NIST 800-92 and 800-137 for additional guidance in security event monitoring.

4.1. In a complex computing environment and faced with dynamic threats and vulnerabilities, it is not practical within the standard to enumerate all security-related events necessary to support the activities for alerting and incident response. Rather, the Responsible Entity determines which computer generated events are necessary to log, provide alerts and monitor for their particular BES Cyber System environment.

Specific security events already required in Version 4 of the CIP Standards carry forward in this version. This includes access attempts at the Electronic Access Points, if any have been identified for a BES Cyber Systems. Examples of access attempts include: (i) blocked network access attempts, (ii) successful and unsuccessful remote user access attempts, (iii) blocked network access attempts from a remote VPN, and (iv) successful network access attempts or network flow information.

User access and activity events include those events generated by Cyber Assets within the Electronic Security Perimeter that have access control capability. These types of events include: (i) successful and unsuccessful authentication, (ii) account management, (iii) object access, and (iv) processes started and stopped.

It is not the intent of the SDT that if a device cannot log a particular event that a TFE must be generated. The SDT's intent is that if any of the items in the bulleted list (for example, user logouts) can be logged by the device then the entity must log that item. If the device does not have the capability of logging that event, the entity remains compliant.

4.2. Real-time alerting allows the cyber system to automatically communicate events of significance to designated responders. This involves configuration of a communication mechanism and log analysis rules. Alerts can be configured in the form of an email, text message, or system display and alarming. The log analysis rules can exist as part of the operating system, specific application or a centralized security event monitoring system. On one end, a real-time alert could consist of a set point on an RTU for a login failure, and on the other end, a security event monitoring system could provide multiple alerting communications options triggered on any number of complex log correlation rules.

The events triggering a real-time alert may change from day to day as system administrators and incident responders better understand the types of events that might be indications of a cyber-security incident. Configuration of alerts also must balance the need for responders to know an event occurred with the potential inundation of insignificant alerts. The following list includes examples of events a Responsible Entity should consider in configuring real-time alerts:

- Detected known or potential malware or malicious activity

- Failure of security event logging mechanisms

- Login failures for critical accounts

- Interactive login of system accounts

- Enabling of accounts

- Newly provisioned accounts

- System administration or change tasks by an unauthorized user

- Authentication attempts on certain accounts during non-business hours

- Unauthorized configuration changes

- Insertion of removable media in violation of a policy

4.3. Logs that are created under Part 4.1 are to be retained on the applicable Cyber Assets or BES Cyber Systems for at least 90 days. This is different than the evidence retention period called for in the CIP standards used to prove historical compliance. For such audit purposes, the entity should maintain evidence that shows that 90 days were kept historically. One example would be records of disposition of event logs beyond 90 days up to the evidence retention period.

4.4. Reviewing logs at least every 15 days (approximately every two weeks) can consist of analyzing a summarization or sampling of logged events. NIST SP800-92 provides a lot of guidance in periodic log analysis. If a centralized security event monitoring system is used, log analysis can be performed top-down starting with a review of trends from summary reports. The log review can also be an extension of the exercise in identifying those events needing realtime alerts by analyzing events that are not fully understood or could possibly inundate the real-time alerting.

Requirement R5:

Account types referenced in this guidance typically include:

- Shared user account: An account used by multiple users for normal business functions by employees or contractors. Usually on a device that does not support Individual User Accounts.

- Individual user account: An account used by a single user.

- Administrative account: An account with elevated privileges for performing administrative or other specialized functions. These can be individual or shared accounts.

- System account: Accounts used to run services on a system (web, DNS, mail etc). No users have access to these accounts.

- Application account: A specific system account, with rights granted at the application level often used for access into a Database.

- Guest account: An individual user account not typically used for normal business functions by employees or contractors and not associated with a specific user. May or may not be shared by multiple users.

- Remote access account: An individual user account only used for obtaining Interactive Remote Access to the BES Cyber System.

- Generic account: A group account set up by the operating system or application to perform specific operations. This differs from a shared user account in that individual users do not receive authorization for access to this account type.

5.1. Reference the Requirement's rationale.

5.2. Where possible, default and other generic accounts provided by a vendor should be removed, renamed, or disabled prior to production use of the Cyber Asset or BES Cyber System. If this is not possible, the passwords must be changed from the default provided by the vendor. Default and other generic accounts remaining enabled must be documented. For common configurations, this documentation can be performed at a BES Cyber System or more general level.

5.3. Entities may choose to identify individuals with access to shared accounts through the access authorization and provisioning process, in which case the individual authorization records suffice to meet this Requirement Part. Alternatively, entities may choose to maintain a separate listing for shared accounts. Either form of evidence achieves the end result of maintaining control of shared accounts.

5.4. Default passwords can be commonly published in vendor documentation that is readily available to all customers using that type of equipment and possibly published online.

The requirement option to have unique password addresses cases where the Cyber Asset generates or has assigned pseudo-random default passwords at the time of production or installation. In these cases, the default password does not have to change because the system or manufacturer created it specific to the Cyber Asset.

5.5. Interactive user access does not include read-only information access in which the configuration of the Cyber Asset cannot change (e.g. front panel displays, web-based reports, etc.). For devices that cannot technically or for operational reasons perform authentication, an entity may demonstrate all interactive user access paths, both remote and local, are configured for authentication. Physical security suffices for local access configuration if the physical security can record who is in the Physical Security Perimeter and at what time.

Technical or procedural enforcement of password parameters are required where passwords are the only credential used to authenticate individuals. Technical enforcement of the password parameters means a Cyber Asset verifies an individually selected password meets the required parameters before allowing the account to authenticate with the selected password. Technical enforcement should be used in most cases when the authenticating Cyber Asset supports enforcing password parameters. Likewise, procedural enforcement means requiring the password parameters through procedures. Individuals choosing the passwords have the obligation of ensuring the password meets the required parameters.

Password complexity refers to the policy set by a Cyber Asset to require passwords to have one or more of the following types of characters: (1) lowercase alphabetic, (2) uppercase alphabetic, (3) numeric, and (4) non-alphanumeric or "special" characters (e.g. #, $, @, &), in various combinations.

5.6. Technical or procedural enforcement of password change obligations are required where passwords are the only credential used to authenticate individuals. Technical enforcement of password change obligations means the Cyber Asset requires a password change after a specified timeframe prior to allowing access. In this case, the password is not required to change by the specified time as long as the Cyber Asset enforces the password change after the next successful authentication of the account. Procedural enforcement means manually changing passwords used for interactive user access after a specified timeframe.

5.7. Configuring an account lockout policy or alerting after a certain number of failed authentication attempts serves to prevent unauthorized access through an online password guessing attack. The threshold of failed authentication attempts should be set high enough to avoid false-positives from authorized users failing to authenticate. It should also be set low enough to account for online password attacks occurring over an extended period of time. This threshold may be tailored to the operating environment over time to avoid unnecessary account lockouts.

Entities should take caution when configuring account lockout to avoid locking out accounts necessary for the BES Cyber System to perform a BES reliability task. In such cases, entities should configure authentication failure alerting.

...

Rationale for R5:

To help ensure that no authorized individual can gain electronic access to a BES Cyber System until the individual has been authenticated, i.e., until the individual's logon credentials have been validated. Requirement R5 also seeks to reduce the risk that static passwords, where used as authenticators, may be compromised.

Requirement Part 5.1 ensures the BES Cyber System or Cyber Asset authenticates individuals that can modify configuration information. This requirement addresses the configuration of authentication. The authorization of individuals is addressed elsewhere in the CIP Cyber Security Standards. Interactive user access does not include read-only information access in which the configuration of the Cyber Asset cannot change (e.g. front panel displays, web-based reports, etc.). For devices that cannot technically or for operational reasons perform authentication, an entity may demonstrate all interactive user access paths, both remote and local, are configured for authentication. Physical security suffices for local access configuration if the physical security can record who is in the Physical Security Perimeter and at what time.

Requirement Part 5.2 addresses default and other generic account types. Identifying the use of default or generic account types that could introduce vulnerabilities has the benefit ensuring entities understand the possible risk these accounts pose to the BES Cyber System. The Requirement Part avoids prescribing an action to address these accounts because the most effective solution is situation specific, and in some cases, removing or disabling the account could have reliability consequences.

Requirement Part 5.3 addresses identification of individuals with access to shared accounts.

This Requirement Part has the objective of mitigating the risk of unauthorized access through shared accounts. This differs from other CIP Cyber Security Standards Requirements to authorize access. An entity can authorize access and still not know who has access to a shared account. Failure to identify individuals with access to shared accounts would make it difficult to revoke access when it is no longer needed. The term "authorized" is used in the requirement to make clear that individuals storing, losing, or inappropriately sharing a password is not a violation of this requirement.

Requirement 5.4 addresses default passwords. Changing default passwords closes an easily exploitable vulnerability in many systems and applications. Pseudo-randomly system generated passwords are not considered default passwords.

For password-based user authentication, using strong passwords and changing them periodically helps mitigate the risk of successful password cracking attacks and the risk of accidental password disclosure to unauthorized individuals. In these requirements, the drafting team considered multiple approaches to ensuring this requirement was both effective and flexible enough to allow Responsible Entities to make good security decisions. One of the approaches considered involved requiring minimum password entropy, but the calculation for true information entropy is more highly complex and makes several assumptions in the passwords users choose. Users can pick poor passwords well below the calculated minimum entropy.

The drafting team also chose to not require technical feasibility exceptions for devices that cannot meet the length and complexity requirements in password parameters. The objective of this requirement is to apply a measurable password policy to deter password cracking attempts, and replacing devices to achieve a specified password policy does not meet this objective. At the same time, this requirement has been strengthened to require account lockout or alerting for failed login attempts, which in many instances better meets the requirement objective.

The requirement to change passwords exists to address password cracking attempts if an encrypted password were somehow attained and also to refresh passwords which may have been accidentally disclosed over time. The requirement permits the entity to specify the periodicity of change to accomplish this objective. Specifically, the drafting team felt determining the appropriate periodicity based on a number of factors is more effective than specifying the period for every BES Cyber System in the Standard. In general, passwords for user authentication should be changed at least annually. The periodicity may increase in some cases. For example, application passwords that are long and pseudo-randomly generated could have a very long periodicity. Also, passwords used only as a weak form of application authentication, such as accessing the configuration of a relay may only need to be changed as part of regularly scheduled maintenance.

The Cyber Asset should automatically enforce the password policy for individual user accounts. However, for shared accounts in which no mechanism exists to enforce password policies, the Responsible Entity can enforce the password policy procedurally and through internal assessment and audit.

Requirement Part 5.7 assists in preventing online password attacks by limiting the number of guesses an attacker can make. This requirement allows either limiting the number of failed authentication attempts or alerting after a defined number of failed authentication attempts. Entities should take caution in choosing to limit the number of failed authentication attempts for all accounts because this would allow the possibility for a denial of service attack on the BES Cyber System.

APPENDIX E

■ ■ ■

NIST 800 Guidelines

The National Institute of Standards and Technology (NIST) material in this appendix is taken from the NIST Computer Security Division Computer Security Resource Center web site. I have included it as a convenient compliance resource since it is referred to in Chapter 8 and other places throughout the book.

The set of guidelines published by NIST is highly regarded. Although it is less frequently cited for compliance than it is for regulatory standards, it is always a good source of security suggestions.

The NIST web page for IT security includes the Special Publications (SP) 800 series. I have selected those articles that most relate to web application security and identified their titles and SP numbers for your reference.

The most relevant publications are SP 800-95, *Guide to Secure Web Services*, and SP 800-44, Version 2, *Guidelines on Securing Public Web Servers*. Other relevant NIST publications are shown in the following list in the order of their SP numbers:

- **SP 800-40, Rev.3**: *Guide to Enterprise Patch Management Technologies*

- **SP 800-83, Rev. 1**: *Guide to Malware Incident Prevention and Handling for Desktops and Laptops*

- **SP 800-100**: *Information Security Handbook: A Guide for Managers*

- **SP 800-102**: *Recommendation for Digital Signature Timeliness*

- **SP 800-111**: *Guide to Storage Encryption Technologies for End User Devices*

- **SP 800-113**: *Guide to SSL VPNs*

- **SP 800-115**: *Technical Guide to Information Security Testing and Assessment*

- **SP 800-118**: *DRAFT Guide to Enterprise Password Management*

- **SP 800-122**: *Guide to Protecting the Confidentiality of Personally Identifiable Information (PII)*

- **SP 800-123**: *Guide to General Server Security*

- **SP 800-128**: *Guide to Security-Focused Configuration Management of Information Systems*

- **SP 800-132**: *Recommendation for Password-Based Key Derivation* "Part 1: Storage Applications"

These publications can be found on the "Special Publications (800 Series)" page in NIST's Computer Security Resource Center: http://csrc.nist.gov/publications/PubsSPs.html.

NIST's drafts of computer-security publications are an additional valuable reference source offered by the institute. These drafts are not necessarily directly related to web application security, but some are closely related. You can find the documents on the "Drafts" page in the Computer Security Resource Center: http://csrc.nist.gov/publications/PubsDrafts.html#SP-800-118.

APPENDIX F

Payment Card Industry (PCI) Data Security Standard Template for Report on Compliance for use with PCI DSS v3.0

This appendix includes excerpts from the "Template for Report on Compliance for use with PCI DSS v3.0" as they provide a convenient compliance resource. The Payment Card Industry Data Security Standard (PCI DSS) is referenced in Chapter 8 and other places throughout the book.[1] For clarity and brevity, only excerpts from the template that most closely align with web application security are shown. For more comprehensive information about the PCI DSS or the "Template for Report on Compliance," you can contact the PCI Security Standards Council directly.

Maintain a Vulnerability Management Program

Requirement 5: Protect all systems against malware and regularly update anti-virus software or programs

PCI DSS Requirements and Testing Procedures	Reporting Instruction
5.1 Deploy anti-virus software on all systems commonly affected by malicious software (particularly personal computers and servers).	
5.1 For a sample of system components including all operating system types commonly affected by malicious software, verify that anti-virus software is deployed if applicable anti-virus technology exists.	• **Identify the sample** of system components selected (including all operating system types commonly affected by malicious software).
	• *For each item in the sample,* **describe how** anti-virus software was observed to be deployed.
5.1.1 Ensure that anti-virus programs are capable of detecting, removing, and protecting against all known types of malicious software.	

5.1.1 Review vendor documentation and examine antivirus configurations to verify that anti-virus programs:
  ○ Detect all known types of malicious software,
  ○ Remove all known types of malicious software, and
  ○ Protect against all known types of malicious software.
(Examples of types of malicious software include viruses, Trojans, worms, spyware, adware, and rootkits).
	• Identify the vendor documentation reviewed to verify that anti-virus programs:
	  ○ Detect all known types of malicious software,
	  ○ Remove all known types of malicious software, and
	  ○ Protect against all known types of malicious software.

	• **Describe how** anti-virus configurations were examined to verify that anti-virus programs:
	• Detect all known types of malicious software,
	• Remove all known types of malicious software, and
	• Protect against all known types of malicious software.

(continued)

6.1 Establish a process to identify security vulnerabilities, using reputable outside sources for security vulnerability information, and assign a risk ranking (for example, as "high," "medium," or "low") to newly discovered security vulnerabilities. *Note: Risk rankings should be based on industry best practices as well as consideration of potential impact. For example, criteria for ranking vulnerabilities may include consideration of the CVSS base score, and/or the classification by the vendor, and/or type of systems affected.* *Methods for evaluating vulnerabilities and assigning risk ratings will vary based on an organization's environment and risk assessment strategy. Risk rankings should, at a minimum, identify all vulnerabilities considered to be a "high risk" to the environment. In addition to the risk ranking, vulnerabilities may be considered "critical" if they pose an imminent threat to the environment, impact critical systems, and/or would result in a potential compromise if not addressed. Examples of critical systems may include security systems, public-facing devices and systems, databases, and other systems that store, process, or transmit cardholder data.*	
6.1.a Examine policies and procedures to verify that processes are defined for the following: ○ To identify new security vulnerabilities. ○ To assign a risk ranking to vulnerabilities that includes identification of all "high risk" and "critical" vulnerabilities. ○ To include using reputable outside sources for security vulnerability information.	• **Identify** the documented policies and procedures examined to confirm that processes are defined: ○ To identify new security vulnerabilities. ○ To assign a risk ranking to vulnerabilities that includes identification of all "high risk" and "critical" vulnerabilities. ○ To include using reputable outside sources for security vulnerability information.

6.3 Develop internal and external software applications (including web-based administrative access to applications) securely, as follows: • In accordance with PCI DSS (for example, secure authentication and logging). • Based on industry standards and/or best practices. • Incorporate information security throughout the software development life cycle. *Note: This applies to all software developed internally as well as bespoke or custom software developed by a third party.*	
6.3.a Examine written software development processes to verify that the processes are based on industry standards and/or best practices.	• **Identify** the document that defines software development processes based on industry standards and/or best practices.
	• **Identify** the industry standards and/or best practices used.

(continued)

6.3.b Examine written software development processes to verify that information security is included throughout the life cycle.	• **Identify** the documented software development processes examined to verify that information security is included throughout the life cycle.
6.3.c Examine written software development processes to verify that software applications are developed in accordance with PCI DSS.	• **Identify** the documented software development processes examined to verify that software applications are developed in accordance with PCI DSS.
6.3.d Interview software developers to verify that written software development processes are implemented.	• **Identify** the software developers interviewed for this testing procedure.
	• For the interview, **summarize the relevant details discussed** to verify that written software development processes are implemented.
6.3.1 Remove development, test and/or custom application accounts, user IDs, and passwords before applications become active or are released to customers.	
6.3.1 Examine written software-development procedures and interview responsible personnel to verify that pre-production and/or custom application accounts, user IDs and/or passwords are removed before an application goes into production or is released to customers.	• **Identify** the documented software-development processes examined to verify processes define that pre-production and/or custom application accounts, user IDs and/or passwords are removed before an application goes into production or is released to customers.
	• **Identify** the responsible personnel interviewed for this testing procedure.
	• For the interview, **summarize the relevant details discussed** to confirm that preproduction and/or custom application accounts, user IDs and/or passwords are removed before an application goes into production or is released to customers.

(*continued*)

6.3.2 Review custom code prior to release to production or customers in order to identify any potential coding vulnerability (using either manual or automated processes) to include at least the following:

- Code changes are reviewed by individuals other than the originating code author, and by individuals knowledgeable about code review techniques and secure coding practices.
- Code reviews ensure code is developed according to secure coding guidelines.
- Appropriate corrections are implemented prior to release.
- Code review results are reviewed and approved by management prior to release.

Note: This requirement for code reviews applies to all custom code (both internal and public-facing), as part of the system development life cycle.

Code reviews can be conducted by knowledgeable internal personnel or third parties. Public-facing web applications are also subject to additional controls, to address ongoing threats and vulnerabilities after implementation, as defined at PCI DSS Requirement 6.6.

(*continued*)

6.3.2.a Examine written software development procedures and interview responsible personnel to verify that all custom application code changes must be reviewed (using either manual or automated processes) as follows:
 	
  ○ Code changes are reviewed by individuals other than the originating code author, and by individuals who are knowledgeable in code review techniques and secure coding practices.
 	
  ○ Code reviews ensure code is developed according to secure coding guidelines (see PCI DSS Requirement 6.5).
 	
  ○ Appropriate corrections are implemented prior to release.
 	
  ○ Code-review results are reviewed and approved by management prior to release.
	• **Identify** the documented software-development processes examined to verify processes define that all custom application code changes must be reviewed (using either manual or automated processes) as follows:
	
	  ○ Code changes are reviewed by individuals other than the originating code author, and by individuals who are knowledgeable in code review techniques and secure coding practices.
	
	  ○ Code reviews ensure code is developed according to secure coding guidelines (see PCI DSS Requirement 6.5).
	
	  ○ Appropriate corrections are implemented prior to release.
	
	  ○ Code-review results are reviewed and approved by management prior to release.

	• **Identify** the responsible personnel interviewed for this testing procedure who confirm that all custom application code changes are reviewed as follows:
	
	  ○ Code changes are reviewed by individuals other than the originating code author, and by individuals who are knowledgeable in code-review techniques and secure coding practices.
	
	  ○ Code reviews ensure code is developed according to secure coding guidelines (see PCI DSS Requirement 6.5).
	
	  ○ Appropriate corrections are implemented prior to release.
	
	  ○ Code-review results are reviewed and approved by management prior to release.

	• **Describe how** all custom application code changes must be reviewed, including whether processes are manual or automated.

(continued)

6.3.2.b Select a sample of recent custom application changes and verify that custom application code is reviewed according to 6.3.2.a, above.	• **Identify the sample** of recent custom application changes selected for this testing procedure.
	For each item in the sample, **describe how** code review processes were observed to verify custom application code is reviewed as follows:
	• Code changes are reviewed by individuals other than the originating code author.
	• Code changes are reviewed by individuals who are knowledgeable in code-review techniques and secure coding practices.
	• Code reviews ensure code is developed according to secure coding guidelines (see PCI DSS Requirement 6.5).
	• Appropriate corrections are implemented prior to release.
	• Code-review results are reviewed and approved by management prior to release.

6.4.1 Separate development/test environments from production environments, and enforce the separation with access controls.	
6.4.1.a Examine network documentation and network device configurations to verify that the development/test environments are separate from the production environment(s).	• **Identify** the network documentation that illustrates that the development/test environments are separate from the production environment(s).
	• **Describe how** network device configurations were examined to verify that the development/test environments are separate from the production environment(s).
6.4.1.b Examine access controls settings to verify that access controls are in place to enforce separation between the development/test environments and the production environment(s).	• **Identify** the access control settings examined for this testing procedure.
	• **Describe how** the access control settings were examined to verify that access controls are in place to enforce separation between the development/test environments and the production environment(s).

(continued)

6.4.2 Separation of duties between development/test and production environments.	
6.4.2 Observe processes and interview personnel assigned to development/test environments and personnel assigned to production environments to verify that separation of duties is in place between development/test environments and the production environment.	• **Identify** the personnel assigned to development/test environments interviewed who confirm that separation of duties is in place between development/test environments and the production environment. • **Identify** the personnel assigned to production environments interviewed who confirm that separation of duties is in place between development/test environments and the production environment. • **Describe how** processes were observed to verify that separation of duties is in place between development/test environments and the production environment.

6.4.5.3.b For custom code changes, verify that all updates are tested for compliance with PCI DSS Requirement 6.5 before being deployed into production.	• **Identify** the sample of system components selected for this testing procedure. • *For each item in the sample,* **identify** the sample of custom code changes and the related change control documentation selected for this testing procedure. • **Describe how** the custom code changes were traced back to the identified related change control documentation to verify that the change control documentation for each sampled custom code change includes evidence that all updates are tested for compliance with PCI DSS Requirement 6.5 before being deployed into production.
6.4.5.4 Back-out procedures.	
6.4.5.4 Verify that back-out procedures are prepared for each sampled change.	• *For each change from 6.4.5.b,* **describe how** the changes were traced back to the identified related change control documentation to verify that back-out procedures are prepared for each sampled change and present in the change control documentation for each sampled change.

(continued)

6.5 Address common coding vulnerabilities in software-development processes as follows:

- Train developers in secure coding techniques, including how to avoid common coding vulnerabilities, and understanding how sensitive data is handled in memory.
- Develop applications based on secure coding guidelines.

Note: The vulnerabilities listed at 6.5.1 through 6.5.10 were current with industry best practices when this version of PCI DSS was published. However, as industry best practices for vulnerability management are updated (for example, the OWASP Guide, SANS CWE Top 25, CERT Secure Coding, etc.), the current best practices must be used for these requirements.

Note: Requirements 6.5.1 through 6.5.6, below, apply to all applications (internal or external):

6.5.1 Injection flaws, particularly SQL injection. Also consider OS Command Injection, LDAP and XPath injection flaws as well as other injection flaws.

6.5.1 Examine software development policies and procedures and interview responsible personnel to verify that injection flaws are addressed by coding techniques that include: ○ Validating input to verify user data cannot modify meaning of commands and queries. ○ Utilizing parameterized queries.	*For the interviews at 6.5.d,* **summarize the relevant interview details** that confirm processes are in place, consistent with the software development documentation at 6.5.d, to ensure that injection flaws are addressed by coding techniques that include: • Validating input to verify user data cannot modify meaning of commands and queries. • Utilizing parameterized queries.

6.5.2 Buffer overflow.

6.5.2 Examine software development policies and procedures and interview responsible personnel to verify that buffer overflows are addressed by coding techniques that include: ○ Validating buffer boundaries. ○ Truncating input strings.	*For the interviews at 6.5.d,* **summarize the relevant interview details** that confirm processes are in place, consistent with the software development documentation at 6.5.d, to ensure that buffer overflows are addressed by coding techniques that include: • Validating buffer boundaries. • Truncating input strings.

(continued)

6.5.3 Insecure cryptographic storage.	

6.5.3 Examine software development policies and procedures and interview responsible personnel to verify that insecure cryptographic storage is addressed by coding techniques that:
 	
   ○ Prevent cryptographic flaws.
 	
   ○ Use strong cryptographic algorithms and keys.
	For the interviews at 6.5.d, **summarize the relevant interview details** that confirm processes are in place, consistent with the software development documentation at 6.5.d, to ensure that insecure cryptographic storage is addressed by coding techniques that:
	
	   • Prevent cryptographic flaws.
	
	   • Use strong cryptographic algorithms and keys.

6.5.4 Insecure communications.	

6.5.4 Examine software development policies and procedures and interview responsible personnel to verify that insecure communications are addressed by coding techniques that properly authenticate and encrypt all sensitive communications.	*For the interviews at 6.5.d,* **summarize the relevant interview details** that confirm processes are in place, consistent with the software development documentation at 6.5.d, to ensure that insecure communications are addressed by coding techniques that properly:
	
	   • Authenticate all sensitive communications.
	
	   • Encrypt all sensitive communications.

6.5.7 Examine software development policies and procedures and interview responsible personnel to verify that cross-site scripting (XSS) is addressed by coding techniques that include:
 	
   ○ Validating all parameters before inclusion.
 	
   ○ Utilizing context-sensitive escaping.
	For the interviews at 6.5.d, **summarize the relevant interview details** that confirm processes are in place, consistent with the software development documentation at 6.5.d, to ensure that cross-site scripting (XSS) is addressed by coding techniques that include:
	
	   • Validating all parameters before inclusion.
	
	   • Utilizing context-sensitive escaping.

(*continued*)

6.5.8 Improper access control (such as insecure direct object references, failure to restrict URL access, directory traversal, and failure to restrict user access to functions).	

6.5.8 Examine software development policies and procedures and interview responsible personnel to verify that improper access control—such as insecure direct object references, failure to restrict URL access, and directory traversal—is addressed by coding technique that include:
 	
   ○ Proper authentication of users.
   ○ Sanitizing input.
   ○ Not exposing internal object references to users.
   ○ User interfaces that do not permit access to unauthorized functions.
	For the interviews at 6.5.d, **summarize the relevant interview details** that confirm processes are in place, consistent with the software development documentation at 6.5.d, to ensure that improper access control is addressed by coding techniques that include:
	
	• Proper authentication of users.
	
	• Sanitizing input.
	
	• Not exposing internal object references to users.
	
	• User interfaces that do not permit access to unauthorized functions.

6.5.9 Cross-site request forgery (CSRF).	
6.5.9 Examine software development policies and procedures and interview responsible personnel to verify that cross-site request forgery (CSRF) is addressed by coding techniques that ensure applications do not rely on authorization credentials and tokens automatically submitted by browsers.	*For the interviews at 6.5.d,* **summarize the relevant interview details** that confirm processes are in place, consistent with the software development documentation at 6.5.d, to ensure that cross-site request forgery (CSRF) is addressed by coding techniques that ensure applications do not rely on authorization credentials and tokens automatically submitted by browsers.

(*continued*)

6.5.10 Broken authentication and session management.

Note: Requirement 6.5.10 is a best practice until June 30, 2015, after which it becomes a requirement.

6.5.10 Examine software development policies and procedures and interview responsible personnel to verify that broken authentication and session management are addressed via coding techniques that commonly include:	**Indicate whether** this ROC is being completed prior to June 30, 2015. **(yes/no)**
○ Flagging session tokens (for example cookies) as "secure." ○ Not exposing session IDs in the URL. ○ Incorporating appropriate time-outs and rotation of session IDs after a successful login.	*If "yes" AND the assessed entity does not have this in place ahead of the requirement's effective date, mark the remainder of 6.5.10 as "Not Applicable."* *If "no" OR if the assessed entity has this in place ahead of the requirement's effective date, complete the following:*
	For the interviews at 6.5.d, **summarize the relevant interview details** that confirm processes are in place, consistent with the software development documentation at 6.5.d, to ensure that broken authentication and session management are addressed via coding techniques that protect credentials and session IDs, including:
	• Flagging session tokens (for example cookies) as "secure".
	• Not exposing session IDs in the URL.
	• Implementing appropriate time-outs and rotation of session IDs after a successful login

(continued)

6.6 For public-facing web applications, address new threats and vulnerabilities on an ongoing basis and ensure these applications are protected against known attacks by either of the following methods:

- Reviewing public-facing web applications via manual or automated application vulnerability security assessment tools or methods, at least annually and after any changes.

Note: This assessment is not the same as the vulnerability scans performed for Requirement 11.2.

- Installing an automated technical solution that detects and prevents web-based attacks (for example, a web application firewall) in front of public-facing web applications, to continually check all traffic.

6.6 For *public-facing* web applications, ensure that *either* one of the following methods is in place as follows: ○ Examine documented processes, interview personnel, and examine records of application security assessments to verify that public-facing web applications are reviewed—using either manual or automated vulnerability security assessment tools or methods—as follows: – At least annually. – After any changes. – By an organization that specializes in application security. – That, at a minimum, all vulnerabilities in Requirement 6.5 are included in the assessment. – That all vulnerabilities are corrected. – That the application is re-evaluated after the corrections.	• For each public-facing web application, **identify which** of the two methods are implemented: ○ Web application vulnerability security assessments, AND/OR ○ Automated technical solution that detects and prevents web-based attacks, such as web application firewalls. *If application vulnerability security assessments are indicated above*: • **Describe** the tools and/or methods used (manual or automated, or a combination of both). • **Identify** the organization(s) confirmed to specialize in application security that is performing the assessments. • **Identify** the documented processes that were examined to verify that public-facing web applications are reviewed using the tools and/or methods indicated above, as follows: ○ At least annually. ○ After any changes. ○ By an organization that specializes in application security. ○ That, at a minimum, all vulnerabilities in Requirement 6.5 are included in the assessment. ○ That all vulnerabilities are corrected ○ That the application is re-evaluated after the corrections.

(continued)

191

○ Examine the system configuration settings and interview responsible personnel to verify that an automated technical solution that detects and prevents web-based attacks (for example, a web-application firewall) is in place as follows: – Is situated in front of public-facing web applications to detect and prevent web-based attacks. – Is actively running and up-to-date as applicable. – Is generating audit logs. – Is configured to either block web-based attacks, or generate an alert.	• **Identify** the responsible personnel interviewed who confirm that public-facing web applications are reviewed, as follows: ○ At least annually. ○ After any changes. ○ By an organization that specializes in application security. ○ That, at a minimum, all vulnerabilities in Requirement 6.5 are included in the assessment. ○ That all vulnerabilities are corrected. ○ That the application is re-evaluated after the corrections.
	• **Identify** the records of application security assessments examined for this testing procedure.
	• **Describe how** the records of application security assessments were examined to verify that public-facing web applications are reviewed as follows: ○ At least annually. ○ After any changes. ○ By an organization that specialized in application security. ○ That at a minimum, all vulnerabilities in requirement 6.5 are included in the assessment. ○ That all vulnerabilities are corrected. ○ That the application is re-evaluated after the corrections.

(continued)

192

	If an automated technical solution that detects and prevents web-based attacks (for example, a web-application firewall) is indicated above:
	• **Describe** the automated technical solution in use that detects and prevents web-based attacks.
	• **Identify** the responsible personnel interviewed who confirm that the above automated technical solution in use to detect and prevent web-based attacks is in place as follows: ○ Is situated in front of public-facing web applications to detect and prevent web-based attacks. ○ Is actively running and up-to-date as applicable. ○ Is generating audit logs. ○ Is configured to either block web-based attacks, or generate an alert.
	Identify the system configuration settings examined for this testing procedure.
	Describe how the system configuration settings were examined to verify that the above automated technical solution is use to detect and prevent web-based attacks is in place as follows:
	○ Is situated in front of public-facing web applications to detect and prevent web-based attacks.
	○ Is actively running and up-to-date as applicable.
	○ Is generating audit logs.
	○ Is configured to either block web-based attacks, or generate an alert.

(*continued*)

193

8.1.8 If a session has been idle for more than 15 minutes, require the user to re-authenticate to re-activate the terminal or session.	
8.1.8 For a sample of system components, inspect system configuration settings to verify that system/session idle time out features have been set to 15 minutes or less.	• **Identify** the sample of system components selected for this testing procedure.
	• *For each item in the sample,* **describe how** system configuration settings were inspected to verify that system/session idle time out features have been set to 15 minutes or less.
8.2 In addition to assigning a unique ID, ensure proper user-authentication management for non-consumer users and administrators on all system components by employing at least one of the following methods to authenticate all users: • Something you know, such as a password or passphrase. • Something you have, such as a token device or smart card. • Something you are, such as a biometric.	

8.2 To verify that users are authenticated using unique ID and additional authentication (for example, a password/phrase) for access to the cardholder data environment, perform the following:
  – Examine documentation describing the authentication method(s) used.
  – For each type of authentication method used and for each type of system component, observe an authentication to verify authentication is functioning consistent with documented authentication method(s).
	• **Identify** the document describing the authentication method(s) used that was reviewed to verify that the methods require users to be authenticated using a unique ID and additional authentication for access to the cardholder data environment.

	• **Describe** the authentication methods used (for example, a password or passphrase, a token device or smart card, a biometric, etc.) for each type of system component.
	For each type of authentication method used and for each type of system component, **describe how** the authentication method was observed to be:
	• Used for access to the cardholder data environment.
	• Functioning consistently with the documented authentication method(s).

(continued)

8.2.1 Using strong cryptography, render all authentication credentials (such as passwords/phrases) unreadable during transmission and storage on all system components.	
8.2.1.a Examine vendor documentation and system configuration settings to verify that passwords are protected with strong cryptography during transmission and storage.	• **Identify** the vendor documentation reviewed for this testing procedure.
	• **Identify** the sample of system components selected.
	• *For each item in the sample,* **describe how** system configuration settings were examined to verify that passwords are protected with strong cryptography during **transmission**.
	• *For each item in the sample,* **describe how** system configuration settings were examined to verify that passwords are protected with strong cryptography during *storage*.
8.2.1.b For a sample of system components, examine password files to verify that passwords are unreadable during storage.	• *For each item in the sample at 8.2.1.a,* **describe how** password files were examined to verify that passwords are unreadable during storage.
8.2.1.c For a sample of system components, examine data transmissions to verify that passwords are unreadable during transmission.	• *For each item in the sample at 8.2.1.a,* **describe how** password files were examined to verify that passwords are unreadable during transmission.
8.2.1.d Additional procedure for service providers: Observe password files to verify that customer passwords are unreadable during storage.	• *Additional procedure for service providers:* **for each item in the sample at 8.2.1.a,** **describe how** password files were examined to verify that customer passwords are unreadable during storage.
8.2.1.e Additional procedure for service providers: Observe data transmissions to verify that customer passwords are unreadable during transmission.	• *Additional procedure for service providers:* **for each item in the sample at 8.2.1.a,** **describe how** password files were examined to verify that customer passwords are unreadable during transmission.

(continued)

8.2.2 Verify user identity before modifying any authentication credential—for example, performing password resets, provisioning new tokens, or generating new keys.	
8.2.2 Examine authentication procedures for modifying authentication credentials and observe security personnel to verify that, if a user requests a reset of an authentication credential by phone, e-mail, web, or other non-face-to-face method, the user's identity is verified before the authentication credential is modified.	• **Identify** the document examined to verify that authentication procedures for modifying authentication credentials define that if a user requests a reset of an authentication credential by a non-face-to-face method, the user's identity is verified before the authentication credential is modified.
	• **Describe** the non-face-to-face methods used for requesting password resets.
	• **Describe how** security personnel were observed to verify that if a user requests a reset of an authentication credential by a non-face-to-face method, the user's identity is verified before the authentication credential is modified.

The complete version of the material found in this appendix is available at following the PCI URL: www.pcisecuritystandards.org/documents/PCI_DSS_v3_ROC_Reporting_ Templatev1.1.pdf.

APPENDIX G

■ ■ ■

Sarbanes-Oxley Security Compliance Requirements

I have included this admittedly very short appendix for the Sarbanes–Oxley Act (SOX) because it is widely cited for IT security compliance. The act is referred to in Chapter 8 and other places throughout the book.

As strange as it may seem, the Sarbanes-Oxley Act does not specify any details for web application security whatsoever. Two organizations, the Committee of Sponsoring Organizations of the Treadway Commission (COSO) and ISACA, stepped up to the plate and created some nontechnical guidelines to interpret IT security requirements for compliance with SOX. COSO has created guidelines, which, in turn, refer to the ISACA COBIT standard. I have taken the next step and refer to the COBIT5 for Information Security standard as the most meaningful COBIT reference for this book.

The two sections of SOX that are pertinent to IT security are Section 302 and Section 404:

Section 302 – Accurate Reporting

Section 302 states that the Chief Executive Officer (CEO) and Chief Financial Officer (CFO) must personally certify that financial reports are accurate and complete. They must also assess and report on the effectiveness of internal controls around financial reporting. This section clearly places responsibility for accurate financial reporting on the highest level of corporate management. CEOs and CFOs now face the potential for criminal fraud liability. It is noteworthy that section 302 does not specifically list which internal controls must be assessed.

Section 404 - Annual Assessment of Internal Controls

Section 404 states that a corporation must assess the effectiveness of its internal controls and report this assessment annually to the SEC. The assessment must also be reviewed and judged by an outside auditing firm. The impact of section 404 is substantial in that a large amount of resources are needed for compliance. A comprehensive review of all internal controls related to financial reporting is a daunting task. As with section 302, the wording of section 404 is broad and does not provide specific guidance as to which controls must be assessed.

It is apparent that no prescriptive recommendations are made for IT security or, by extension, for web application security. Nonetheless, as mentioned previously, SOX is often cited as a compliance requirement for IT security audits.

A SANS article describing the interrelationships between SOX, COSO, and COBIT cites the two standards noted previously, COSO and COBIT, as governing the IT security for SOX.

COSO is more general in nature than COBIT, and COBIT5, which is discussed in this book, is the most relevant of the COBIT collection of standards for the purposes of SOX compliance.

A good source of information about the Sarbanes-Oxley Act is the SEC web site:

```
www.sec.gov/about/laws/soa2002.pdf
```

For information about the COSO framework, you can go to the COSO organization's site:

```
www.coso.org/documents/COSO%20McNallyTransition%20Article-Final%20COSO%20
Version%20Proof_5-31-13.pdf
```

Details of COBIT5 for Information Security can be found in Appendix A of this book.

The source for the SANS content in this appendix is found at Institute Infosec Reading Room in "An Overview of Sarbanes-Oxley for the Information Security Professional":

```
www.sans.org/reading-room/whitepapers/legal/overview-sarbanes-oxley-
information-security-professional-1426
```

APPENDIX H

Sources of Information

(ISC)², "Ten Best Practices for Secure Software Development"

www.isc2.org/uploadedFiles/(ISC)2_Public_Content/Certification_Programs/
CSSLP/ISC2_WPIV.pdf

On the web site of the International Information Systems Security Certification Consortium, or (ISC)2, you will find this article about the best practices for securely developing applications.

(ISC)², The *Official (ISC)² Guide to the CISSP CBK*, 3rd Edition
This training guide is for the (ISC)² CISSP certification exam. It contains a lot of material relevant to information security.

Harold F. Tipton and Steven Hernandez, *Official (ISC)²
Guide to the CISSP CBK*, 3rd Edition (Boca Raton, FL: CRC)

ISACA, "Common Web Application Vulnerabilities"

www.isaca.org/Journal/Past-Issues/2005/Volume-4/Pages/Common-Web-
Application-Vulnerabilities1.aspx

This page on ISACA's web site explains common types of web application security risks and the associated best practices to avoid them.

Microsoft, "Basic Security Practices for Web Applications"

http://msdn.microsoft.com/en-us/library/zdh19h94(v=vs.100).aspx

This page on the Microsoft Developer Network web site is about good security practices for developing and managing web applications.

NIST, National Vulnerability Database

http://web.nvd.nist.gov/view/vuln/search

On the National Institute of Standards and Technology's web site, you will find the National Vulnerability Database, where you can search for software flaws (CVEs) and misconfigurations (CCEs).

OWASP, "2013 Top 10 List"

www.owasp.org/index.php/Top_10_2013-Top_10

This web page the Open Web Application Security Project (OWASP) web site identifies the top 10 most critical web application security flaws and links to tables identifying relevant factors for each, such as threat agents and attack vectors.

OWASP, "Secure Coding Cheat Sheet"

www.owasp.org/index.php/Secure_Coding_Cheat_Sheet

This page on the OWASP web site pertains to how to securely code a web site.

OWASP, "Web Application Firewall"

www.owasp.org/index.php/Web_Application_Firewall

This page on the OWASP site is about web application firewall technology.

SANS Institute, "Framework for Secure Application Design and Development"

www.sans.org/reading_room/whitepapers/application/framework-secure-
application-design-development_842

This page from the SANS Institute Reading Room site addresses the practice of secure application design and development, and presents a framework to assist developers.

Stanford University, "State of the Art: Automated Black-Box Web Application Vulnerability Testing"

http://theory.stanford.edu/~jcm/papers/pci_oakland10.pdf

This paper, published on the Stanford Theory Group site, describes vulnerability scanners used for testing web applications.

University of California, "Secure Coding Practice Guidelines"

https://security.berkeley.edu/content/application-software-security-
guidelines?destination=node/403

This page on the Berkeley Security web site pertains to secure coding practices.

University of Pennsyvania, "Top 10 Web Application Security Vulnerabilities"

www.upenn.edu/computing/security/swat/SWAT_Top_Ten_A8.php

This page on the Penn Computing web site describes what it considers to be the top 10 web application security vulnerabilities.

Index

A

Access control, 27, 54
  audit observation, 29
  cached HTTP response, 55
  cached HTTPS response, 28
  character set/charset, 29, 57
  clickjacking attack, 27–28
  discretionary access control, 77
  disclosing unnecessary information, 56
  frameable response, 55
  HTML comments, 28, 56
  insecure cookies, 30, 58
  mandatory access control, 77
  session expiration, 29, 57
  session fixation, 58
Annual loss expectancy (ALE), 114
Application security, 111
  ALE, 114
  business case, 119
  prevention and remediation, 115
  residual risk measurement
    cost-justifying remediation and
      calculation, 124
    cost of, mitigation, 126
    effectiveness of, mitigation, 127
    monthly security health
      scorecard, 123–124
    remediating *vs.* fixing, 125
  risk assessment
    identification, business
      impact, 112
    likelihood of occurrence, 113
    qualitative and quantitative risk
      analysis, 113–114
  security investment
    budget, 116
    calculation, 116
      projected *vs.* actual cost of
        losses, 129
      web-application-security breach,
        straw poll, 116–117, 119
Authentication
  brute-force method, 23
  encryption, 50
  harvesting, 50
  password controls, 22, 49
  requirements, 48
  unencrypted
    connection, 23

B

Brute-force attacks, 34, 62

C

Clickjacking attack, 27–28
Compliance, 99
  expert organization, 101
  financial auditors, 102
  government regulations, 100
  industry standards, 100
  logical approach, 107
  requirements, 107
  security standards, 106
Cookies, 30
  client-side code, 32
  domain attribute, 32
  HttpOnly flag, 31
  prolonged expiration, 31
  secure flag, 31
CRAMM method, 4
Cross-site request forgery
  (CSRF), 43, 74

Cross-site scripting (XSS) attacks
    CSRF, 43
    reflected XSS, 41
    stored XSS, 42

■ D

Data masking, 76
Denial-of-service (DoS) attacks, 44
Discretionary access controls (DACs), 77
DREAD model, 4–5

■ E

Error handling, 40–41
Experian EI3PA security, 147
    anti-virus updation, 151
    develop and maintain secure
        systems, 152
    encrypt transmission, 150
    hacker communities, 148
    network resources, access, 157
    PCI SSC materials, 147
    testing, 158
Extended enterprise architecture
        framework (E2AF), 128

■ F, G, H

Facilitated risk analysis process
        (FRAP), 4
Federal Enterprise Architecture (FEA), 128
Framework, secure code, 85
    application testing, 89
    backups, 85
    error handling, 88
    HttpOnly flag, 87
    indirect file path, 87
    input validation, 88
    management buy-in, 85
    monitoring and alerts, 86
    output encoding, 88
    password management, 86
    patching, 86
    secure flag, 87
    security team, 85
    separation of duties/environments, 85
    session management, 87
    SSL/TLS, 87
    training, 89
    verification, 88

■ I, J, K, L

Injection flaws, 62
    active directory, 38
    blind SQL injection, 36, 64
    hidden directory, 39
    HTTP header injection, 36, 65
    HTTP response-splitting attack, 36, 66
    internal IP address, 39
    link injection, 65
    obsolete servers, 40
    server path, 39
    source code, 37
    SQL injection, 35, 63
    SSL request, 40
    temporary files, 39
    VIEWSTATE, 40
    web directory, 38
IT security risks
    breach, 2
    calculation models
        CRAMM, 4
        DREAD, 4–5
        facilitated risk analysis process
            (FRAP), 4
        OCTAVE Allegro, 4
        spanning tree analysis, 4
        STRIDE, 4
    calculations, 6
        customized approach, 7
        monetary value, 9
        multiple threats, 9
        security risk, 8
    compromise, 2
    countermeasure, 3
    mitigation, 3
    relative risk, 2
    residual risk, 3
    risk, 1
    temporal risk, 2
    threat, 2
    vulnerabilities, 2, 10
IT security standards
    appendices, 103
    COBIT, 103
    E13PA, 104–105
    ISO 105, 27000
    NERC CIP, 105
    NIST, 105
    PCI DSS, 104
    Sarbanes–Oxley act, 106

■ M

Mandatory access controls (MACs), 77

■ N

National Vulnerability Database (NVD), 10
North American Electric Reliability Corporation's Critical Infrastructure Protection standard (NERC CIP), 105

■ O, P, Q

OCTAVE Allegro, 4
Open Web Application Security Project (OWASP), 10

■ R

Real-life vulnerabilities, 21
    access control, 27
        audit observation, 29
        cached HTTPS response, 28
        character set, 29
        clickjacking attack, 27–28
        HTML comments, 28
        insecure cookies, 30
        session expiration, 29
    authentication
        brute-force method, 23
        passwords, 22
        unencrypted connection, 23
    cross-site scripting (XSS) attacks, 41
        CSRF, 43
        stored XSS, 42
        reflected XSS, 41
    denial-of-service (DoS) attacks, 44
    error handling, 40–41
    injection flaws
        active directory, 38
        blind SQL injection, 36
        hidden directory, 39
        HTTP header injection, 36
        HTTP response-splitting attack, 36
        internal IP address, 39
        obsolete servers, 40
        server path, 39
        source code, 37
        SQL injection, 35
        SSL request, 40
        temporary files, 39
        VIEWSTATE, 40
        web directory, 38
    input validation, 32
        buffer overflows, 33
        GET method, 34
        parameter manipulation attack, 33
        script execution, 32
    redirects and forwards, 34
    security issues, 44
        account lists, 45
        data at rest, 44
        password storage, 45
        patch management, 45
    security misconfigurations, 43
    session management, 23
        GET method, 25
        harvesting, 26
        hashing, 24
        internet security, 26
        session ID/token/identifier, 27
        SSL, 24–25
        stored credentials, 26
        TCP, 24
        TLS, 24
        UDP, 24
    unauthorized data view, 37
ROSI, 116

■ S

Secure sockets layer (SSL), 24
Software-development life cycle (SDLC) process
    business requirements, 82
    change management, 84
    code development, 83
    code testing, 84
    design phase, 83
    framework, secure code (see Framework, secure code)
    integration and validation, 84
    policy, secure code, 83
    production, 84
    security requirements, 82
    threat modelling, 83
Spanning tree analysis, 4
STRIDE model, 4

■ T

Testing, 13, 89
  audit process, 14
  automate-code tools, 90
    dynamic-code analysis, 92
    static-code analysis, 91
  multilayered defense, 93
  penetration testing, 14, 17
  postremediation testing, 14, 18
  reports, 18
    audit reports, 18
    testing reports, 18
  vulnerability testing, 14–15
    automated testing, 15, 17
    manual testing, 16–17
Third-party software, 95
  change management, 97
  liability insurance, 97
  transparency of problem resolution, 95
Transmission control protocol (TCP), 24
Transport layer security (TLS), 24

■ U

US Computer Emergency Readiness Team
  (US CERT), 10
User datagram protocol (UDP), 24

■ V

Vulnerability remediations, 47
  access controls, 54
    cached HTTP response, 55
    character set/charset, 57
    disclosing unnecessary
      information, 56
    frameable response, 55
    HTML comments, 56
    insecure cookies, 58
    session expiration, 57
    session fixation, 58
  authentication, 48
    encryption, 50
    harvesting, 50
    password controls, 49
    requirements, 48
  cross-site scripting (XSS) attacks, 72
    CSRF, 74
    reflected XSS, 72
    stored XSS, 73

  denial-of-service attack, 75
  injection flaws, 62
    blind SQL injection, 64
    HTTP header injection, 65
    HTTP response-splitting attack, 66
    link injection, 65
    SQL injection, 63
  input validation, 59
    active code, 59
    buffer overflows, 60
    GET method, 61
    unauthorized access, 60
  redirects and forwards, 61
    brute-force attacks, 62
  security issues, 76
    account lists, 77
    data at rest, 77
    password storage, 78
    patch management, 78
  security misconfigurations, 75
  session management, 50
    data storage, 52
    error messages, 53
    GET method, 52
    HTML forms, 53
    POST method, 52
    random session ID, 53
    secure socket layer (SSL), 51
  unauthorized data view, 67
    active directory, 68
    error handling, 71
    hidden directory, 70
    internal IP address, 69
    obsolete server, 70
    server path, 69
    source code, 67
    SSL request, 71
    temporary files, 69
    VIEWSTATE, 70
    web directories, 68

■ W, X, Y, Z

Web application firewall (WAF), 93
Web application security
  issues, 131
  IT group, 131
  process, 131
  risk mitigation, 132
Web Application Security Consortium
  (WASC), 10

Get the eBook for only $10!

Now you can take the weightless companion with you anywhere, anytime. Your purchase of this book entitles you to 3 electronic versions for only $10.

This Apress title will prove so indispensible that you'll want to carry it with you everywhere, which is why we are offering the eBook in 3 formats for only $10 if you have already purchased the print book.

Convenient and fully searchable, the PDF version enables you to easily find and copy code—or perform examples by quickly toggling between instructions and   applications. The MOBI format is ideal for your Kindle, while the ePUB can be utilized on a variety of mobile devices.

Go to www.apress.com/promo/tendollars to purchase your companion eBook.